C000015464

Employee Engagement

a little book of Big Ideas

Jasmine Gartner, PhD

TINYBIG

London

Published 2015 by TINYBIG Books

Copyright 2015 © Jasmine Gartner

All rights reserved. No part of this book may be reprinted or reproduced or utilised in any form or by any electronic, mechanical, or other means, now known or hereafter invented, including photocopying and recording, or in any information storage or retrieval system, without permission in writing from the author or publisher.

British Library Cataloguing in Publication Data
A catalogue record for this book is available from the British Library.

ISBN 978-0-9931366-0-3

Contents

Introduction
Making the Case for Employee Engagement:
The Five Spheres

The world of work is changing.

Think about all the new ways of working. These days, going to work doesn't mean being in the office from 9 to 5. It could include flex-time, working from home, or desk shares.

Technology is also rapidly changing the landscape of the workplace. Twenty years ago, who could have imagined the impact applications like LinkedIn or Facebook would have?

But, it's not just how we define the workplace that's changing. Peoples' ideas about what they should get from work are changing.

People are starting to expect more than a pay packet from work. They want choice and voice. They want a place to work that they can be proud of – they want to work for an employer of choice. Sir Ken Robinson, an expert on creativity in education, has suggested that being 'in your element' not only means being good at what you do, but loving it[1].

---

[1] Sir Ken Robinson, *Finding Your Element: How to Discover Your Talents and Passions and Transform Your Life*. New York: Penguin Books. 2013.

If the world of work is changing, then this means that ideas about how to engage employees have to evolve too.
And ideas about engagement are indeed evolving.

Historically, engagement was seen as something somewhat divorced from organisational strategy. It was aimed at individual satisfaction at work. So for example, the *Sunday Times 100 Best Companies to Work for* listed an overwhelming number of drivers, including family friendliness, health and safety, job interest, feeling valued, co-operation, and equal opportunities, amongst many others.

In 2009, this was streamlined and aligned with organisational strategy by the MacLeod Report[2], which was commissioned by the then Labour government. The MacLeod report specified that there were just four drivers of employee engagement: strategic narrative, engaging managers, employee voice, and organisational integrity.

MacLeod's drivers are spot-on, in terms of what the business ought to do. Of course you need a strong strategic narrative, and engaging managers, with a robust organisational culture, and employees should have a voice in this.

Generally speaking, though, the implication has been that engagement is something companies do *to* employees, rather than *with* them – it certainly doesn't seem to be something that employees themselves do.

My view is that the future of employee engagement must be a symbiotic relationship between employer and employee, where both must actively work together to reap the benefits.

---

[2] David Macleod and Nita Clarke. 'Engage for Success.'
http://www.engageforsuccess.org/wp-content/uploads/2012/09/file52215.pdf

The goal is to get people – employers, employees – involved, participating, creating and communicating. Engagement should mean that businesses benefit in terms of productivity, greater degrees of harmony, and enhanced levels of interaction and communication. Engagement should mean that employees benefit in terms of greater job satisfaction and fulfilment at work.

A Definition of Employee Engagement

There are many definitions of employee engagement. This makes perfect sense as each workplace will have different problems and therefore will need different engagement solutions. That said, we can still define the areas where engagement happens and what it means in those contexts.

First of all, I want to be clear that the term "employee" includes managers. All employees – managers and staff – have to work together to ensure a successful company, which in turn, continues to provide employment for all.

Secondly, let's identify where engagement – or disengagement – happens. Employee engagement takes place through relationships between the worker and:

o The company –in terms of organisational culture and values, and its organisational strategy for success

o The work itself – how an employee sees the work that needs to be done – is it valued and necessary? The work itself includes knowledge, skills and aptitudes, but also takes into account personalities and connections needed to get the job done

o The team – people may work with the same team or be a member of different teams. This includes what configurations work best for people to help them to achieve company goals; it also includes how people ask for and give help to each other

o The network – how people interact with different teams or companies, as well as the people they are networked with outside work. Workers are at the nexus of a network of people at work and beyond work, professional and social. The network also includes clients or customers.

o   Society (or the social environment) – we are affected by the outside world in terms of culture, but also in terms of the major and minor events that take place which may influence our lives and business. This includes politics, legislation, and general cultural values.

I call these the *Five Spheres of Employee Engagement.*

So here is the working definition I'll be using:

Optimum employee engagement is when employee and employer move fluidly amongst these five spheres, actively and appropriately matching skills, knowledge and experience to enhance and improve the workplace. In this way, the goals of individual and organisation can be balanced and achieved.

It is possible for a worker to be engaged with any combination of these spheres. At one advocacy organisation, for example, there is a disconnect between staff and management. Staff feel that they are untrusted and left out of the loop. However, they are fully engaged with the work they do with their clients.

I'm suggesting that we have to move towards a more nuanced and complex understanding of employee engagement. We have to move away from the assembly line mentality definition of engagement – the employee is there to do a job, and only their skill and ability to get that job done is important.

In other words, employee engagement doesn't happen when an employer hires a skill set, separate from the human being. A skill set cannot successfully navigate the five spheres; only a self-aware human being can.

So, engagement is about the organisation asking the whole person to come to work, not just his or her ability to do a specific job.

And, in keeping with that, it's asking that that person take responsibility for his or her life at work, just like they would outside of work.

Benefits of Engagement for Different Stakeholders
Let's take a look at the benefits of engagement for organisation and individual.

The Employer's point of view
What business problems does engagement solve? Why bother throwing resources at what seems to be a woolly concept?

It's important to put this notion of engagement as woolly or politically correct to rest. Organisations, such as Gallup and the Civil Service[3], have done research that has shown that the UK loses upwards of £60 billion a year due to disengaged staff. Clearly, then, engagement is not a woolly concept, and it has a clear and large impact on the bottom line.

Engagement is good from a business perspective – we know from research that highly engaged workers are much more productive, and this inevitably affects businesses' bottom line. This positive feedback loop also means that a space is opened up for creativity and innovation, which again feeds right back into improving business as usual.

One good reason, then, to engage staff is that it is a way to maximise profitability through increasing productivity. This has a knock on effect on retention of staff, absenteeism, and customer focus and satisfaction.

---

[3] http://www.engageforsuccess.org/wp-content/uploads/2012/09/file52215.pdf

These, then, are some of the other benefits of engagement for organisations in terms of the five spheres:

The company:
- Lower employee turnover and lower recruitment costs
- People understand how strategy affects them and can engage with it
- Belief in organisation

The team:
- Development of team / personal goals linked to corporate goals
- Teams more effective at setting goals

The network:
- Self-nominated opt-in to strategy and culture, on the part of all staff
- Access to more information / knowledge from a broad range of participants

The work itself:
- Higher knowledge retention, leading to better work decisions
- More purposeful goal-setting, as work goals are integrated with strategy
- Continuous improvement is embedded in culture

Society:
- Improved corporate reputation for customers and staff, and for potential customers and staff (employer of choice)
- Slowly changing the way society works – for the better – changing the culture of how we live
- It's in everyone's best interest to build an economy of engaged people

From the Employee's point of view

The rewards for the employee are huge. Job satisfaction, upskilling and CPD are just a part of the picture, where people are encouraged to develop expertise. By unlocking people's potential, and asking the whole person to come to work, employees start to feel valued and respected.

If an organisation succeeds in engaging its workers, then the worker will also bring those feelings of achievement outside the workplace, so that creativity and innovation at work may well impact on creativity and innovation outside of work.
This is particularly relevant for knowledge workers, whose creativity and innovative ideas may be why they were hired.

When the whole person comes to work, great things happen:
The company:
- o People want to come to work
- o People feel valued and respected
- o Staff feel they can make a difference
- o Staff feel they are being treated fairly
- o Employees report an increased sense of well-being as well as lower feelings of stress

The team:
- o People have a greater scope to make decisions
- o Employees become more confident
- o People know what they're good at and opt-in to projects that they can improve
- o People become more responsible and accountable to their colleagues

The network:
- o Networks strengthen through improved channels of communication
- o External networks become strengthened
- o Team work, collaboration and problem-solving lead to innovation and creativity on a broader level

The work itself:

- o Individuals actively take part in their own development, identifying areas for improvement which are in keeping with organisational strategy and culture
- o People are more responsible and accountable for achieving their goals at work

Society:

- o Creativity and critical thinking are encouraged and flourish
- o Diversity and inclusivity are reinforced and advanced
- o As the workplace improves, those mores are translated outside work and slowly are embedded within the culture at large

Conclusion

Employee engagement is a clever move for business. There's nothing woolly about it.

It should be an essential part of every organisation's strategy. Because, if correctly identified and implemented, employee engagement can provide a competitive edge to business.

The challenge lies in analysing the Five Spheres, and aligning them successfully with organisational strategy and culture.

This book comes in two parts:

Part One examines the Five Spheres in detail, with a chapter dedicated to each one. We'll look at what obstacles each sphere puts in the way of engagement, and what the strategies and solutions are.

Part Two is a toolkit for sowing the seeds of engagement in your own workplace. After having read Part One and understanding the context for engagement – the part that addresses the question 'why do it?' – Part Two helps you to tailor this approach to your business.

PART ONE:

The Five Spheres

Chapter 1: Save us from Boredom
The First Sphere - Engaging with the Company

> ➤ *Is there a link between engagement and productivity?*
> ➤ *Is the company responsible for the happiness of individual employees?*

In 2005, I took a job as the assistant to a financial director in a small company in New York. In many ways, it was a perfect job for me. Not only was the pay decent, but I was paid hourly, so I only needed to work when there was work to do. And, I really got along well with the financial director, which is very important, as Marcus Buckingham points out in *First, Break All the Rules*[1]: people, he says, leave managers, not jobs. It was a good thing we got along too, seeing as we shared a small, windowless office, with our desks adjacent to each other. We had similar temperaments and an abiding love of a strong coffee first thing in the morning.

The financial director – let's call him Bob – had been brought in to get the company into shape so it could be sold, and the woman who had started it could retire. Essentially, he had to transform it from an inefficient husband-and-wife-run organisation to a profitable – and therefore saleable – company. For the first six months or so, this arrangement was very good. There was so much work for me to do. But as both

---

[1] Marcus Buckingham. *First, Break All the Rules*. London: Pocket Books. 2005.

of us were very efficient, and very hard workers, we managed to get our department into shape very quickly..

Once everything was organised, once routines were in place and contacts made, the work itself levelled off. What had started as a four-day a week job quickly became less and less. But, I still needed to make a certain amount of money, and Bob still wanted to have his assistant there, for when any unexpected – but rare – tasks might come up. Not only did I get my "real" work done, but I also organised our closet, I cleaned up and updated our files and filing system. I tweaked things, fixed whatever I could. I was the first to offer to run errands, no matter how trivial. I'd go to the bank, I'd go buy office supplies (even though we could have done that on-line), and I'd go out to buy us coffee. But the truth was that at some point, there was too little real work for me to do. I tried to pace myself, but I am not very good at working slowly.

And that's when the problem started. I started to be bored at work. This wasn't the lovely lingering childhood boredom of long summer days, the boredom which nurtures creativity. No, this was instead the boredom that gave birth to anxiety and unhappiness.

I didn't skive off too much – don't forget, Bob sat immediately next to me, so there really was no hiding what I was doing. But I would read the paper for a bit when I arrived in the morning. I might take a few extra trips to the water cooler. An extra coffee in the afternoon seemed increasingly like a good idea. I might do a bit of research for the classes I was teaching, if Bob stepped out of the office. It was nothing terrible, and that way I could still answer the phone and I was there to deal with any issues that might arise, if need be.

I am sure that I am like many workers. Of course, I wanted to make Bob happy, but there simply wasn't enough for me to do. I would happily have done more. I also had to balance that with the necessity of making enough money to pay the rent on my flat, and my desire to save for the future. And I made no link between what I did and how the company performed. I did all my work, after all, and I did it well.

This was compounded by the way the owners of the company worked. As far as I could tell, this husband and wife team showed little regard for their workers – a feeling that was reinforced by other employees, with whom I'd chat at the water cooler or in the break room. I saw no less than three employees lose their jobs – they'd learn of it and be out the same day. The owners would talk with disrespect of some employees, and show a complete lack of understanding of the rest of us. The husband gave all the women employees a stuffed animal on Valentine's Day. The intention may have been good, but in a small company, it came across as patronising at best, and sexist at worst. Imagine if he had given all the men little toy soldiers. It would have been considered strange and inappropriate to treat them as children.

If it weren't for Bob, whom I greatly respected and with whom I continued to have a good relationship, the owners' attitude would have had a deeply negative impact upon my work ethic. As it was, I worked to earn his respect, not theirs.

This situation wasn't good either for me or for the company.

What does Boredom at Work Look Like?
David Bolchover cites some worrisome figures in his 2005 book, *The Living Dead*, about what office workers get up to.

"46% of holiday online shopping takes place at work," he says. "Almost 40% of workers in the UK, Germany and the US spend an hour or more every day e-mailing their friends and relatives via their company e-mail system during working hours."

He points out a 2002 survey in the UK, which found that 30% of small and medium sized companies lose "more than a day's work per week to Internet surfing and personal e-mail use, costing this sector of the economy an estimated total of £1.5 billion per year."[2]

That same year, another survey of 30,000 workers in the US found that 1 in 5 respondents "had had sex with a co-worker during work hours... 44% of men and 35% of women have had at least some sexual contact at work."[3]

Bolchover's stats go on and on. Drug use at work? Yes. Internet porn? Yes. Sickies? Yes. Sleeping at one's desk? Yes. A 2004 poll found that 24% of respondents fell asleep "either at their desk, in a meeting or in the toilet," whilst another 39% said that they didn't sleep at their desks, but certainly had trouble staying awake.[4]

Try googling the expression "bored at work," to see how creative people are in their attempts to while away time in the office. You can start with www.boredatwork.com - a list of sites, as the site's tagline says, to "fight off work-related boredom." Or what about www.nothingtodo.co.uk? Then there are many sites dedicated to games, videos and humour. www.i-resign.com has a history of boredom for people who are bored at work. Then there are the companies whose adverts let you know that they can help you with your boredom – some radio stations, the music magazine NME, a few self-help blogs. www.zenhabits.net says "just find things to entertain yourself." The author lists a whole host of things to do to alleviate boredom – from doing crunches to finding a hobby to reading blogs. In fact, you have to ask yourself – if there was no such thing as boredom at work, what would the Internet look like?

---

[2] David Bolchover. *The Living Dead: Switched Off, Zoned Out*. Sussex: Capstone Publishing Company. 2005, 36.

[3] Bolchover, 6

[4] Bolchover, 6

All of these percentages and statistics focus on what the employee is or isn't doing at work. This raises a big question: does this mean that disengagement and the subsequent loss of profit to the company are the worker's fault?

The Cost of Disengagement
Engagement is a two-way street. Yet more often than not, that two-way street ends up being a maze of vicious circles, where the driver of worker boredom is perceived to be people trying to take advantage or get away with something, and in turn, when the organisation tries to control these behaviours, it is seen as Big Brother. No wonder there is so much mistrust between the two types of employees – managers and staff.

While the way people cope with boredom at work might sound more or less harmless, if annoying for the employer, it actually has a shocking financial cost to any organisation. And if the cost of disengagement is high financially for the organisation, it is also high psychologically for the worker. Extrapolate that to a societal level – organisations losing money hand over fist, and thousands of people wasting time at work, flushing away their lives and their potential. What kind of world do we live in?

Yet the deleterious link between employee habits and organisational well-being seems to be invisible.

As I mentioned in chapter one, disengaged staff cost the UK upwards of £60 billion a year – in the United States, that number is around $355 billion a year.[5] Clearly, skiving off at work is a sign of disengagement, and it's one of the main areas where that revenue is lost.

Yet, as my own example shows, workers are not necessarily out to undermine their companies. They are simply not

---

[5] Macleod.

making the link between their own behaviour and the repercussions of those behaviours for the company. They're also not making the link between their behaviour and the impact it has on their own well-being.

Let's be fair. The exact same thing can be said of managers and chief executives. They also are almost certainly not out to undermine their companies. They too are failing to make the link between their own behaviour and the repercussions of those behaviours on the company. And while there is literature on disengaged managers (who engage in the same boredom-alleviating strategies as any other employee), there is very little about what it is that managers – even engaged managers – do that so effectively disengages other people down the line.

The company has so much to gain from engagement. Engaged employees stay with the organisation, which means lower employee turnover and lower recruitment costs.[6] It also means less absenteeism, as engaged employees are less stressed – and stress is one of the most common of workplace-related illnesses.[7] Engaged employees believe in their organisation, and work to their best ability, if they understand the organisational strategy and how it will help them maintain or improve business as usual.

The individual worker also has a lot to gain from engagement. The benefits range from physical health (engaged staff report an increased sense of well-being as well as lower feelings of stress) to psychological health (engaged staff know they are valued and respected, they know they can make a difference and that they will be treated fairly). In short, engaged people *want to* come to work.

[6] Macleod
[7] 'Stress-related and psychological disorders in Great Britain 2014.'
  http://www.hse.gov.uk/statistics/causdis/stress/index.htm

Having put to rest the idea that employee engagement is a woolly concept, what exactly can organisations do to bring engagement into their workplaces? Engagement in this sphere is different to engagement in the other four spheres – the network, the team, the work itself, and society.

What should the Company be doing to Boost Engagement?

Not only does disengagement cost any organisation a great deal, but actively engaging staff could increase revenue dramatically. The Hay Group found that "organisations in which people feel both motivated and 'enabled' can achieve revenue growth 4.5 times that of peers." Indeed, their 2010 research showed that in the UK, the problem is not entirely due to a lack of staff motivation: close to 75% of UK staff surveyed, they found, were "prepared to 'go the extra mile.'" They just didn't have everything necessary to do their jobs. [8]

This points clearly to the idea that engagement is both a management issue and a staff issue. A more pointed question that we could ask is: What exactly is necessary for people to do their jobs? While managers might be able to provide the answer in terms of the job description, staff need to also tell managers what they need to do their job.

That said, it's important to avoid falling into the trap of the *Times 100 Best Places to Work*, and start listing every possible thing that a person might need in order to do their job – in other words, the wishlist. The result could easily be individual solutions that may help some people – perhaps just the one person – but not everyone. So while some people may need childcare, not everyone does. While some people may want flexible working hours, others might not. People who drive to work will have different needs than those who use public transportation. And, let's not forget that

[8] Graeme Yell. 'Engagement Matters.'
http://www.haygroup.com/EngagementMatters/research-findings/united-kingdom.aspx

needs change over time, so that someone who needs childcare now won't need it forever. As the employee ages, they may have new needs. And so on. Each of these needs will be very important to whomever requested it at the time; but responding to everyone's individual needs will result in the creation of a huge amount of work for the organisation, with uncertain outcomes in terms of engagement.

The Perception of Unfair Treatment – the Wish List

Those outcomes are uncertain because paying attention to individual, subjective needs raises the issue of fairness. It means that people will constantly be comparing what they've got to what other people have received. It adds an element of competition, where there shouldn't be any. If I don't need much in order to do my work, how will I feel when I find out how the company has bent over backwards to provide a lot to a needy member of staff? My initial engagement at being provided with childcare might dim when I find out that somebody else needs a greater number of holidays.

This subjective list of each individual's specifications would mire the organisation in the work it takes to satisfy everyone's idiosyncrasies in order to get them to work. And these would constantly change as people measured up benefits against each other, and found that they weren't getting the same quality or quantity as others. In a big company, these many solutions might help more than one person at a time, but what about in an organisation of 50 people?

Therefore, addressing subjective, individual needs will at best be ineffective; at worst, it will actively cause disengagement.

And in the attempt to make everyone happy, the time remaining for doing the actual work of the organisation would certainly be squeezed. The challenge here is to identify what it is the organisation needs to do to get people involved, without getting trapped in the detail of subjective needs and desires of all the individual staff.

All in all, it seems clear that within the five spheres where someone can engage, the company is not the one that can be tailored to individual needs. As we will see later in this book, there are other spheres where individual needs can be catered to effectively and to positive effect.

Perhaps it's a question of reframing the idea of what is necessary for people to do their jobs. In other words, if engagement looks different depending upon which of the five spheres we're talking about, then perhaps what people need from the company in order to do their jobs is different from what they need in terms of the other spheres.

So, if subjective needs – the wish list – shouldn't drive engagement in terms of the company, what should?

In order to answer this, we really have to take a step back and examine what the overall goals of any organisation are and therefore what engagement should look like, coming from the company sphere.

What Drives Engagement in the Company Sphere?

During engagement workshops, I usually ask employees – managers and staff alike – what they think managers are there to do. The usual response is "they're there to make money." When I ask why, the response is "to keep the business afloat." I ask why again, and it's "to keep the shareholders happy." I ask again, and finally someone will say, "to make sure there is a business going forward." This is the heart of the matter – the organisation's most basic goal is survival. In other words, its most basic goal is to maintain business as usual.

Therefore, a manager's role is to come up with ways to ensure that business as usual is maintained, or – even better – improved. The process looks a bit like this: one day, a manager might be reading a paper, or might be speaking with a colleague at the office, or at a conference, or walking around the shop floor, and she realises that if things stay the way they are, business as usual will suffer. The trigger for change could be any number of things: she could read about new legislation, or notice a sea change in her industry, or something like the credit crisis of 2008 could hit. The list easily goes on: a new competitor might appear in the market, or a natural disaster could hit, like the volcanic ash cloud that hit the tourism industry in northern Europe in 2010. These are all external triggers. Internal triggers could include efficiencies, or the necessity for implementing new technology and the related need to train staff. A new CEO could come on board with a new vision for the company. Roles could change as customer needs change or develop. And so on.

Having noticed a trigger for change, the manager is then concerned about how that trigger could impact upon the business, either positively or negatively. Either way, she comes up with a strategy to address it, to either take advantage of the positive benefits or to mitigate for the negative ones. This kind of flexibility, being able to adapt successfully, will be one of the marks of being a good manager.

To staff this often looks arbitrary. If they don't understand or even see those triggers for change, it just looks like change for change's sake. Yet, their jobs depend upon the ability of managers to successfully navigate an ever-changing world.
This means that all employees – managers included – should be working together to help maintain or improve business as usual. Everyone's future is at stake here, so everyone needs to understand why change is necessary.

Remember that surviving – and doing well – is the company's purpose.

This is why it makes no sense for the company to address individual needs. If the company is bogged down in trying to make individual staff happy, it won't have the time necessary to pay attention to all the external and internal triggers for change that may affect business as usual, and respond to them with appropriate strategies.

Derek Luckhurst, of the IPA, a London-based charity dedicated to best practice in the UK, puts it this way: "It is essential to emphasise, for example, that at work as at home, individual well-being is an individual's responsibility; and, at work, the employer has a responsibility to the individual insofar as he or she is a member of staff as a group. This means that rather than trying to make individual employees happy, an employer must be dedicated to treating employees as a group fairly. Happiness is subjective and orientated towards the individual; fairness is objective and relational, only making sense within the context of a group" (Luckhurst 2008).

When speaking about engagement, then, we should always come back to this idea of business as usual and the all-important ideas of strategy and fairness.

Strategy and Fairness
In fact, one of the biggest causes of disengagement is when staff cannot understand how they plug into the organisational strategy or when they don't understand why what is happening at work has an effect on them.

Let me give you a simple example. Imagine that one day, my manager comes to me and says, "I'm afraid we're cutting your work week by two days, and docking your pay for those two days." Now imagine my response. Is it positive or negative? Am I rational or emotional? Also, imagine the impact on my productivity. It is going to take a dive of major proportions, as I start to think about *why* they're doing this to *me*. What have I done wrong? Is the next step to push me out the front door? As I grow resentful or scared and worried about my future, I'll focus less on work.

But now, imagine this is happening in 2008, when there was a huge financial crisis – by shortening everyone's work week and cutting their pay, the management have come up with a way for everyone to keep their jobs until the crisis is over, rather than creating redundancies. Now imagine my reaction. I might not like that I have lost work, but I certainly understand why it's happened, and why it's happened to me. My productivity might not increase, but it won't nosedive either.

Understanding strategy was all that it took for me to become engaged. This, of course, is the option that quite a few companies chose during that financial crisis.

What about in a more difficult situation – can strategy engage when there is more at stake? After all, in the example I gave above my job wasn't ultimately in danger. So let's take a real world example, which I've heard on a number of occasions.

Let's say, for example, that management go to staff and announce that there will be redundancies made. "The business needs to do this," staff are told, "so that it can stay competitive."

This is a shock.

Staff in the disengaged workplace will tend to feel that they haven't been brought in on a decision that will have a major impact on their lives, and that they are being consulted rather late in the game. Resentful or scared and worried, they may cease working as hard. If before they were just apathetic or slightly disengaged, they become actively disengaged, further driving down the company's productivity. Here the vicious cycle of blame and mistrust create a downward spiral for business as usual.

But if managers were to provide a few extra bits of information, they could avoid the downward spiral. First of all, staff who understand the laws of consultation in the EU, know that a company cannot consult until a decision's been reached that *may* cause redundancies. Straight away, this addresses the concern on the part of staff that they have not been consulted early enough. They now know that their company is obeying the regulations on the subject. They may not *like* it, but they *understand* why the company has behaved in the way it has. Rational analysis slowly starts to replace emotional reaction.

Information and facts provide a rational counterpoint to the emotional guesses that people come up with, as they try to understand how managers got from point A – "we're fine how we are" – to point B – "we must make redundancies."

I call the gap between those two points the **vortex of misinformation** because without the facts, people will try to guess why change is happening and why *they* are directly in its line of fire. In the absence of facts and information, their guesses will be negative, emotional, subjective, and personal – given a vacuum, they will come up with their own stories to explain how the company got from point A to point B. They will become less productive, and as they tell their colleagues and friends their vortex stories as to why change is happening, they will drag others down into the vortex. Those friends and colleagues will also become less productive, once again negatively impacting upon business as usual.

Closing the Vortex with Strategy
It's in everyone's best interest that that vortex is closed up.

The solution is elegant and simple, yet very few organisations take advantage of it.

I learned this solution from the IPA's Derek Luckhurst, mentioned above, and I have worked for him as a trainer for many years, so I was able to see and hear over time how his methods really worked.

As you will no doubt guess, strategy is central to his method. But it's not just that.

His method is predicated upon the idea of *fairness*, which I discussed above. His feeling was that staff who were being affected by change needed to know that they were being treated fairly. More than that, those staff who *weren't* being directly affected by change also needed to know that affected staff were being treated fairly. They needed to know so that the next time change happened, they would think, "I saw how the last process went, when people were treated fairly, so I can expect the same."

And in order for this to happen, people had to understand why change was happening. They had to not only understand strategy, but how that strategy was arrived at.

This is the brilliant part of Luckhurst's approach.

Basically, he stated that it wasn't just the final strategy that staff needed to hear. "Staff," he explained in a 2003 article, "generally have little idea about the options their managers have considered." He continued, "They usually feel that decisions are taken in an ivory tower, with no thought about the effects on them as employees. In a redundancy situation, for example, workers tend to believe the redundancies *are* the business objective – rather than a consequence of it."[9]

In other words, staff need to understand the process from beginning to end, including the triggers for change, and all the other strategies managers looked at before arriving at their preferred option. In order to understand the big picture, staff need to understand why the other strategies were

---

[9] Derek Luckhurst. *Option-Based Consultation Provides Mutual Benefits* 2003.

rejected. This will help them to follow the managers' logic in choosing their preferred option, which should be the one that best addressed the need for change. Only by showing the rejected options, do managers make it clear why their choice is best and that it wasn't the only thing they thought of.

In Luckhurst's model, "The What, the Why, and the What Else" are a series of questions enabling staff to scrutinise management thinking: what were the other options? Why were they rejected? What else did you think of?

Most of the time, it would show staff that there were no grounds for cynicism. Occasionally, of course, it might show up poor decision-making; but then staff suspicions about decision-making would have a basis in fact, and people could make educated and informed decisions about what they wanted to do. They might also realise that managers are human and make mistakes; that, in fact, the managers had not *intentionally* set out to make a bad decision.

By having this information, staff would be using an entirely different tone of voice when they would say, "I bet managers didn't think of...": instead of cynicism, they would now actually be able to see what managers hadn't thought of, and could put options on the table as well, thereby improving the decision-making process.

This approach lays the groundwork for trust, transparency and understanding. Whilst staff might not like how decisions impact on individuals, they should be able to understand how the company as a whole – business as usual – would suffer if changes were not brought in. They would start to understand that in order for the whole company to survive, some individuals would be affected, but more people would benefit positively from this.

Managers also would benefit from this process, as opening up decision-making to scrutiny would help to reinforce good decision-making. Additionally, they might get strategic advice from staff that they might not have thought of.

The key is that everyone needs to understand strategy, or the big picture of why the company works the way it does, and everybody needs to feel that change is fair, rather than a personal attack on staff.

Engagement in the Company Sphere

In this sphere, engagement has been shown to derive from involvement with company strategy: staff may or may not be involved in coming up with strategies, perhaps they will just influence them, or perhaps they will just have all the facts and information at their fingertips so they can understand why change is happening to them – but the bottom line is that they absolutely must understand all the strategies that were considered, and why they were rejected.

If this becomes a widely adopted model, then it has the potential to affect every other sphere of engagement.

Chapter 2
The Second Sphere
The Work Itself and Making your own Engagement

> ➢ *Why is individual achievement essential to how well a business does?*
> ➢ *What are the factors that contribute to an individual's ability to do great work?*

The Relationship between the Worker and the Work Itself

I sat down to write my doctoral dissertation in the very cold, snowy winter of 2002. I would literally spend the first three weeks in a month making myself increasingly ill with anxiety – I couldn't write, but I couldn't do anything else either. By the beginning of the fourth week, I would have made myself so ill I couldn't leave my flat. So I would sit down, snuggled up in a duvet and I would write for a week. At the end of the fourth week, I would have one chapter finished and be miraculously feeling better. Then I would start the process again. It took me six months to write six chapters; if I hadn't had writers' block, it might have taken me six weeks.

Ever heard of writers' block? If you've experienced it, you know it's an incredibly frustrating experience.

You sit, staring at a blank screen or a blank sheet. You stare off into space. Perhaps you do some chores or try to distract yourself. But you feel constantly aware of the fact that there is writing to be done, and that that writing simply is not getting done. You feel discouraged and anxious. You might be someone who, if you're not writing, feels guilty if you do anything else. So you sit there, hunched over, beating yourself up for your failure.

You wonder if this is worth it. Why have you chosen this career? Why?

But then, the day comes – and it always does come – when the fog lifts, and you can suddenly sit down to write. You might write for hours, or days. You are completely focussed, perhaps unaware of anything else going around you. If somebody didn't put food and tea in front of you, you might not remember to eat or drink.

You've achieved a period of what psychologist Mihaly Csikszentmihalyi calls *flow*. In his book of the same title, Csikszentmihalyi defined this seminal idea: "Being completely involved in an activity for its own sake. The ego falls away. Time flies. Every action, movement, and thought follows inevitably from the previous one, like playing jazz. Your whole being is involved, and you're using your skills to the utmost."[1]

When you emerge, the relief you feel is huge. Anxiety drains from your body, to be replaced by a surge of contentment, a feeling like no other.

This is why you do it – this is what makes all the misery that came before worth it.

By the way, the idea of immersing oneself in an activity so as to lose the self has been around for a long time. Usually, though, it's been about art or religion. In India, a long time

---

[1] Mihaly Csikszentmihalyi. *Flow*. London: Rider Books. 2002.

ago, art in the form of theatre and dance were considered sacred because, unlike a painting, they took time to experience. And that time gave people the chance to lose themselves as they were immersed in it. Csikszentmihalyi has brought an ancient idea back into our modern awareness.

I don't think anything could change my process of writing since I'm not *choosing* to be this way. I've always worked this way, since school days, and I imagine I will always work this way. And it's not necessarily a terrible way to be. I'm not desperately trying to figure out how to change how I do things. After all, it seems to work for me. And it works for my employers and clients – I have never missed a deadline yet. Of course, they don't need to know what a close finish it is!

Relationship between the Worker and the Client / Employer

Even if it did make an employer or client nervous that all the writing comes in a brief period after a long time spent not writing, there's not much an employer could do to change it.

A stick or carrot approach would fail, since I'm not sitting there with my arms crossed, thinking, "if only they paid me more..." Punishing me wouldn't work either – in fact, it would just add to the stress already caused by writers' block, and probably delay me even further.

Once posed with the challenge (write something!), my employer (or my client, if I'm freelance) has to let me figure out the way to best achieve it, to get into that state of flow.

In other words, by giving me greater scope to make decisions, and allowing me to choose my own path, I am better able to unlock my own potential. And this makes me feel valued and respected, which takes some of the stress out of my life. I feel trusted to get things done on my own terms, and in turn if I am trusted then I will start to think that what I do makes a real contribution to the company or client who has hired me.

All this is dependent upon knowing me – knowing my boundaries, what makes me tick, and what'll stop me dead in my tracks. And this means I have to be 100% actively participating in my own engagement – if I don't tell people who I am and what I need to work, how can anyone else know these things?

Looking at Engagement from the Wrong Side
People tend to look at engagement from the wrong side.

It's like Christmas time on Oxford Street in London. Walking down that street, thousands of people are looking in shop windows. Perhaps you find yourself staring longingly at the beautiful displays in the windows, thinking about how that dress, those shoes, that piece of furniture – whatever the item is – would be perfect in your wardrobe or flat.

Would it, really though? Those things that look great in the shop window might make no sense at all in my small flat, or with the existing outfits I already own. More than that, I may not be able to afford what I see there, or even if I have the money, I may have to prioritise my spending differently. There are real world constraints that I have to live within.

But I look in the windows, along with everybody else, and I think, "I'd like some of that."

Engagement is a bit similar. Everybody is looking at those organisations who have it (perhaps as they read the *Times 100 Best Places to Work* list), and wistfully, they're saying, "I'd like some of that at my organisation."

But engagement, like material goods, is not one-size-fits-all. You can't necessarily take what works in one place and relocate it to another. Instead of being the person outside, looking longingly into the shop windows, you have to become the window-dresser, choosing elements in alignment with your specific needs and according to your real world constraints.

Because work changes and because life changes, you have to constantly be adapting and reprioritising your needs and desires, as constrained by the real world around you. And this is true of all areas of life, including work. At work, like outside of work, you have to understand the real world constraints and then formulate your priorities within those boundaries. This means you have to identify the constraints placed on you by the organisation in terms of its budget, future goals and strategy, and then you have to use these constraints to contextualise your own needs, such as salary, job satisfaction and your own future goals. Engagement can be found where the needs of the organisation and the needs of the individual worker are in equilibrium.

No workplace is static, and no worker's life is static. Attaining that tenuous equilibrium could be a life-long balancing act.

In the last chapter I mentioned that while the company sphere cannot be dedicated to individual needs, there is another sphere that can. This is it. The trick, though, is that while the organisation can provide the environment for extraordinary work, the individual worker has to then actively tailor this environment to his or her own needs.

In other words, each worker has to develop a strategy for doing his or her own best work. When the environment for great work has been set up and the employee has then tailored that environment, you'll have engagement in the second sphere: the work itself.

Five Steps for Engagement in the Second Sphere
Work itself is different for everyone. But, creating the environment for extraordinary work can be addressed with consistency.

Here are five steps, which should lay the groundwork for any individual to find flow. This is a project that needs the active participation of all employees – staff and managers.

1) *Link organisational strategy to individual lives*
2) *Understand how your work fits in the context of the organisational big picture*
3) *Be self-aware: know your habits, strengths and limits*
4) *Define and articulate your Continuous Professional Development (CPD)*
5) *Build a face-to-face community – be aware of others – know other people's needs and boundaries*

Achieving each of these steps successfully is predicated upon the active involvement of both employee and employer, as I'll explain below in more detail.

Step 1
Link organisational strategy to individual lives

You can't have engaged employees unless they have a clear understanding of organisational strategy, as discussed in chapter 1, about the company sphere.

In other words, the work itself has to be aligned with company strategy. If staff don't clearly understand strategy, then it becomes very difficult for them to decide which of their workplace needs make sense within the overall framework for the business. They need to understand how their work fits into the bigger picture, so everything makes sense and is done for a reason – so timelines, company goals, the company's idea of where it would like to be positioned in the future, how the company is doing financially, and so on, are all necessary pieces of information, which the employee must have to contextualise what the work itself is, why it's necessary and important and when it has to be done by. And this all becomes even more essential during times of change, if employees are to continue to be productive.

A forward-looking company provides this kind of information without asking; in companies that are behind the curve, employees need to be pro-active and ask for it.

Step 2:
Understand your work in the context of the big picture
To get the work done, you need to know the answer to a simple question: "what?" and a more complex one – "how?"

In order to answer the first question, you have to understand organisational strategy, its values, roles and rules, so you can plug your work into that framework. That will allow you to understand why the work you're doing is important, when it needs to be done by, and how it fits into the bigger picture.

Once you know what is expected of you (you know what needs to be done and why), you can ensure that you have the basic materials and equipment. You can start to determine if you need to add or improve on your skills, knowledge and aptitudes to keep up with the organisation's long term goals. Gallup has suggested that being able to address what is expected of you and what materials and equipment you need is the first step in assessing and moving towards engagement.

Answering the more complex question – how? – requires self-awareness on the part of the employee (staff or manager). You've been given the goal; it's up to you to determine how you get there. And this means knowing yourself, and knowing what an optimal work situation is for you.

Most companies provide the answer to the "what" through job descriptions, and therefore provide the necessary tools. But as we've probably all experienced, job descriptions shift and change with time. Again, employees have to be pro-active in addressing these shifts.

And, only the individual employee can answer the "how," letting the employer know about other tools or training he or she might need, or other skills and knowledge he or she brings to the table, which might improve the environment, enabling the employee to do his or her best work.

Step 3:
Be self-aware – know your habits, strengths and limits

Remember Csikzentmihalyi's idea of flow that I mentioned at the beginning of this chapter - "being completely involved in an activity for its own sake"? In order to get to this state, you first have to define your habits, your strengths, and your limits. These things will create the space, which enables flow for you.

Obviously, then, in order to create the right environment for flow, you have to be highly self-aware. You have to ask yourself a series of questions in order to determine and express your habits, strengths and limit.

One woman I know has to have her desk perfectly organised before she can start her work. I have to have a cup of tea at the ready, and some background noise – preferably talk radio, or some music. Some people need to check their email or have a coffee. Habits are part of the routine, of which work is a part. In terms of strengths, it could be the amount of research you do before you're comfortable to start your work. It could be the amount of knowledge, skills and aptitudes you have. It could be the knowledge that you work best in the mornings. Your limits include knowing what gets in the way, what are the obstacles? This might be about your personality type – if you are impatient, perhaps not detail-orientated, and so on.

Some other questions might be: do you need structure and supervision? Or are you self-sufficient? Do you work best first thing in the morning or in the evening? Are you an extrovert or an introvert – in other words, do you need a stimulating environment to work in, or a very quiet peaceful one? Are things taking place outside of work that affect your ability to do your work well? Are there skills or knowledge that you have from your non-work life that could improve what you do? What are your interests outside work? Is there an overlap between what you enjoy when you're not at work and what you do when you are at work?

Once you've identified your own needs and boundaries, you have to communicate them to other people. Assuming that people know what you want, or that they'll treat you the way you want to be treated won't work. Communicate clearly about your needs and boundaries, so you can be managed in the way that makes the most sense for you. This will also be important if you're working as part of a team, which we'll look at in a later chapter. It'll be the way that makes the most sense for the company too, because you'll be helping the company help you to achieve their goals.

(Check out our Self-Awareness at Work Checklist in the last part of this book to start a list of traits that could help your manager manage you in the way you'd like to be managed).

What you have essentially done here is create an environment where the obstacles that normally come between you and getting your work done are either completely removed or minimised. Your work is meaningful (you understand where what you do fits into the bigger picture), and you have the tools necessary to do it. Now it's just a question of doing it.

And while it's obvious that your organisation might profit from this, you as an individual will also profit from it. It's a symbiotic relationship. Therefore, you should have a vested interest in actively working towards creating the right environment for you to do your best work in. In other words, how can you contribute to developing yourself?

Your employer needs to contribute to this by recognising that you're not just a skill set – by getting to know you as a person so that they help create the environment for you as an individual to shine.

Step 4:
Define your Continuous Professional Development
A recent survey carried out in 2011 by Paul Fairlie showed that "No matter what your age, most of us need to work at something that matters to us and the world in general."[2]

Basically, if people are bored at work, they need to work towards finding what makes work interesting; life can be and more often than not is easily filled with mundane routines. Work offers us the chance to carve out a little space where the extraordinary can happen.

The real trick is ensuring that satisfying the worker is also good for the organisation. By understanding both the goals of the organisation you work for, and your own habits, strengths and limitations, you'll also be able to clearly articulate where you need development in order to maintain a level of challenge in your work that is satisfying to you.

Because you'll be able to link this need for development with the goals of the company, it means that your development is good for you but it's also good for the company.

You can come up with targets for your own development that are plugged into organisational strategy, and managers can help their people develop targets too. In fact, a key role for a manager might be to ensure that individual targets are indeed plugged into organisational strategy.

The crucial point here is that these targets are directly related to organisational strategy – so that staff are aligning their

---

[2] Paul Fairlie. 'All Generations Want Meaningful Work.' *HR Reporter* 2011.

needs with making the business work better, and so upskilling becomes mutually beneficial.

Autonomy, Mastery, Purpose

Daniel Pink builds on Csikszentmihalyi's idea of flow in his book *Drive*.[3] He notes that people are much more likely to have "optimal experiences" – Csikszentmihalyi's flow – on the job than during leisure. In fact, Pink challenges the idea that work is, as he says, "*not* inherently enjoyable." This premise feeds much of the business world's approach to motivation. If work isn't inherently enjoyable, then motivation can be derived from reward or punishment to encourage people to do what they don't want to do because it isn't enjoyable.

Pink looks at the research of various scientists on the idea of motivation, which shows that people have an inherent curiosity, which motivates them to work things out. And they enjoy it. He turns the idea that work is "not inherently enjoyable" on its head. In fact, work often provides people with three elements that provide our lives with meaning: autonomy (a desire to be self-directed), mastery (a desire to get better at something) and purpose (to work on something that is bigger than ourselves).

The goal of the worker, who is actively involved in his or her own engagement, should be to find what aspect of work makes it enjoyable for them (autonomy) within the context of organisational strategy (purpose), because that will motivate them to work well (mastery). This varies from person to person, and can apply to almost any kind of work.

The employer's goal should be to help create the environment for the employee that will enable them to find that motivation. Getting to know the habits, strengths and limitations of employees – again, this includes staff and

---

[3] Daniel Pink. *Drive: The Surprising Truth about what Motivates Us*. Edinburgh: Canongate Books. 2010.

managers – is a plus for the employer. It provides an understanding of how employees see themselves fitting in to the big picture, and it will show if and where there has been any breakdown in communication – it's only by having people articulate their understanding of organisational strategy that you can know if they've understood it correctly.

Step 5:
Build a face-to-face community
Chances are, you work in some way or another with other people. If nothing else you have clients or an employer. For work to be produced well, it's important that you can move fluidly amongst the other people you work with, by understanding their habits, strengths and limitations.

This is very different than the idea of the rule, which says that you should treat others as you'd like to be treated.

In fact, that idea of the golden rule is very flawed. Think about it this way: say I'm going to a meeting, and it's early, and I desperately want a cappuccino. Thinking that I'll treat my colleagues the way I want to be treated, I bring everyone a cappuccino. In reality, that wouldn't work – some people might not drink caffeine, some might like something cold, some people might not even be thirsty or want anything at all.

By treating others as I'd like to be treated, I've basically ignored the fact that they are individuals with desires specific to them.

The proper way to do this is to get to know my colleagues well enough that I can treat them the way *they'd* like to be treated, rather than the way *I'd* like to be treated. And this happens when everyone shares his or her habits, strengths and limitations so that the team can work together effectively.

We'll look at the team in more detail in the next chapter.

There's a bit more, though, to it than this: it's not just that the team will work better if everybody knows each other. That's true, and it's useful and important. But there's a big picture element here – even bigger than the workplace, this is about changing the world we live in.

Change Your Attitude, Change the World we Live in

Right now, in our society, there is an approach to work that says that it is a net-sum game – whether that is due to job shortages during recession, or changes in technology (oil and gas replacing coal for example), or social dynamics (perceptions of immigration, for example, or attitudes towards diversity). If I don't have what it takes, someone else will get the job. It pits us, as workers, against each other in a never-ending competition.

This competitive outlook keeps workers on their toes. The excess labour pool that we always have in the West – either people who are unemployed and looking for work, or those on welfare (and of course sometimes the two groups can overlap) – serves two functions.

First, when there is lots of work, there is a ready workforce who are desperate for work and will take on work that is perhaps not as well-paid as it could be, or not an exact match for a given worker's skills. Secondly, by having surplus labour, the desires of those people who do have jobs are kept in check, since they know there are any number of people who would gladly have their jobs, should they ask for too much.[4]

If instead we look at the world of work as made up of self-fulfilling individuals, then there is potentially a place for everyone. Then it is no longer a net-sum game, but instead work can be seen as inherently enjoyable, and working

---

[4] David Harvey. *The Enigma of Capital*. London: Profile Books. 2010.

together as inherently positive. This doesn't mean that people have to like each other; they just have to work together.

A workplace full of individuals who are participating as whole people with a vested interest in their own engagement might be the place to start if we want to plant the seeds of a society that looks out for its own and that moves away from the competitive and towards the truly collaborative.

It wouldn't be the first time. In *The Enigma of Capital*, David Harvey pointed out that workers have been the drivers of change – "the power of labour over the years has yielded concessions over matters such as employment conditions, workplace safety, regulation of social relations (anti-harassment and equal treatment legislation), skill definitions, and the like,"[5] which are all sizeable victories.

As the nineteenth-century American philosopher William James said, "The greatest revolution of our generation is the discovery that human beings, by changing the inner attitudes of their minds, can change the outer aspects of their lives." That's a revolution not just for his generation, but for all of ours. Steve Jobs built on this when he said, "When you grow up you, tend to get told that the world is the way it is and your life is just to live your life inside the world, try not to bash into the walls too much, try to have a nice family, have fun, save a little money. That's a very limited life. Life can be much broader, once you discover one simple fact, and that is that everything around you that you call life was made up by people that were no smarter than you. And you can change it, you can influence it, you can build your own things that other people can use."[6]

---

[5] Harvey, 103

[6] Maria Popova. 'The Secret of Life from Steve Jobs in 46 Seconds.'
http://www.brainpickings.org/2011/12/02/steve-jobs-1995-life-failure/

Conclusion: What Does Engagement do for the Work Itself?
Encouraging creativity and critical thinking by raising self-awareness is obviously good for the individual. But it will also have a direct impact on the bottom line, and eventually, if there is enough of a groundswell, on our societies as well.

By helping people unlock their own potential at work, you open the doors to better quality work because:
• People have a greater scope to make decisions
• People feel valued and respected
• People want to come to work
• People feel they can make a difference

An improved environment for creating work impacts beyond the workplace too:
• People are more confident
• People have a greater sense of well-being
• People have less feelings of stress
• People feel included
• People develop expertise and more freedom – "empowerment"
• People actively engaged in innovating and problem-solving

Basically, allowing for a better workplace through optimising the quality of the work produced creates a set of skills, knowledge and aptitudes that can be carried forward to the family or to other spheres of individual existence, eventually improving society as a whole.

Chapter 3
The Third Sphere
The Team – It's a Small World

> ➢ *How does culture affect business?*
> ➢ *How do teams work?*
> ➢ *What's the ideal size for an effective team?*

Over a hundred years ago, a German sociologist called Ferdinand Tönnies noticed that as society industrialised, he was able to distinguish between two different types of human groups: he noticed that people interact with each other differently, depending upon whether they belonged to a small group or a large one.[1]

Tönnies was analysing the changing landscape of industrialising Europe, as people moved from small family groups, often in rural settings, to the anonymity of the cities. But, his observations are remarkably spot-on when looking at small and large groups in general, or in the case of this book, at work.

In this chapter, I'll look at the impact of small groups on the workplace; in chapter 4, I'll look at the impact of big groups.

---

[1] Ferdinand Tönnies. *Community and Civil Society*. Cambridge: Cambridge University Press. 2001.

Unlike with the first two spheres (the company and the work itself), this is the first time we'll really have to try to understand the importance of culture in the workplace. Why? The first two spheres are about the direct relationship between employer and employee. But this third sphere (and the fourth sphere as well) is about a group of people working together: it's about the team. And anytime that you have a group of people, there will be some form of culture binding them together. Culture, by the way, is just defined as a learned and shared set of rules, roles and behaviours.

We'll discuss what makes a small group cohere: the size, culture and values that provide the ideal environment for engagement.

The Small Group
We've now moved past the first two spheres, which allowed the individual worker to engage with the company through understanding strategy and a feeling of being treated fairly, and create an environment where he or she could produce the best work. Many of us are freelance, but even so, generally we need to work with others.

In the context of work, your organisation might be the large group, while your team is the small group. Or you might work for the local branch of a multinational corporation. We can think of small groups as teams and big groups as networks.

You may not work for a big group. But, chances are – in one way or another – you work as part of a small group. If nothing else, even if you are freelance or work from home, you have clients or an employer.

And it's essential that a small group is put together well and works smoothly. The potential for disengagement is high – a

2008 Gallup article by Jennifer Robson[2] points out that 17% of employees will leave a job because of managers. Another factor for leaving an organisation mentioned in the same article is when an employee perceives that his or her co-workers are not committed to high standards. While pay and benefits are important, so are the relationships between people.

There are all sorts of ways in which a team can go wrong, which will have a deep impact on individual engagement. Strong personalities can overshadow the more reticent, biases might not be overcome, a culture of conformity can silence criticism. Those are just a few examples, there are many more.

For work to be produced well, it's important that you can move fluidly amongst the other people you work with, by understanding your own habits, strengths and limitations, as well as those of your teammates and colleagues.

So what are the ingredients that make a strong team? In short, it's all about personal relationships. From that basic principle, we'll come up with a whole slew of values:
1. Don't follow the Golden Rule (instead, learn about habits, strengths and limits)
2. Identify the ideal workable size of the group (remember, it's based on relationships)
3. Be flexible, take risks and innovate

Don't Follow the Golden Rule of Reciprocity
I mentioned the Golden Rule of Reciprocity in chapter 2: treat others as you would like to be treated. Yet, as I showed, the Golden Rule is a terrible strategy and a great way to make mistakes. The truth is not only should everyone *not* be treated

---

[2] Jennifer Robson. 'Turning Around Employee Turnover.'
http://www.gallup.com/businessjournal/106912/turning-around-your-turnover-problem.aspx 8 May 2008.

the same way, not everybody *wants* to be treated the same way.

In *First, Break All the Rules*, Marcus Buckingham gives the example of an employee, Mark, who didn't want to be recognised for his good work with a meaningless plaque. Yet, his manager, John, did this a few years in a row. It wasn't until John listened to his employee that he was able to reward Mark in the way *he* wanted to be rewarded.[3]

We probably all have examples like this. At a conference I once organised, a colleague of mine drew attention at the end of the day to a woman called Caroline who had given the keynote address. He thanked her and suggested we give her a round of applause. Afterwards, Caroline told me how she absolutely hates that kind of thing. She felt that we had all worked on this together, and that there was no reason to single her out for praise.

As Buckingham puts it, "each employee has his own filter, his own way of interpreting the world around him, and therefore each employee will demand different things... Each employee breathes different psychological oxygen."[4]

The proper way to do this is to get to know your colleagues well enough that you can treat them the way *they'd* like to be treated, rather than the way *you'd* like to be treated. And this happens when everyone shares their habits, strengths and limitations so that the team can work together effectively, formally or informally. That is, as you work on projects with other people in a formal setting, you will start to suss these things out – but also, you can start to forge those personal ties informally – at the water cooler or in the break room.

If you have to be able to know something about each of the people you're working with, this limits the number of people

[3] Buckingham, 2005.
[4] Buckingham, 151.

you can have on a team. Let's start with a basic question: what is the ideal number of people for a team?

Dunbar's Number

Research suggests that any individual can keep tabs on up to 150 people. These 150 or so people form the maximum group size in which people can function well, if they are working together to achieve a goal. A larger group can function well, as long as there isn't a common goal (for example, think of your compatriots – do you all share the same goal? Countries are a good example of large groups that can function well but haven't got the same specific goals).

This is called *Dunbar's Number*.[5] You might have heard of Dunbar's number in regards to Facebook. There have been a number of articles, in magazines like the Economist and New Scientist, which said that no matter how many hundreds of Facebook friends you might have, the upper limit of those you can keep tabs on is 150. The number you actually interact with, with any regularity, is much, much smaller – typically 50. And the number you interact with *often* comes down to about six to fifteen. Six to fifteen members in a group seems to be the optimum number for achieving goals. Think of this in the context of sports teams or army units.

Recently, a colleague with whom I was planning a series of workshops said to me, "let's keep the number of attendees to no more than 12." This was entirely based on her experience – she hadn't heard about Dunbar's number before.

These two aspects – having learned each others' habits, strengths and limitations, and having kept the group small enough that everyone is able to remember these things about each other – are essential aspects to small group culture.

---

[5] Maria Konnikova. 'The Limits of Friendship.'
http://www.newyorker.com/science/maria-konnikova/social-media-affect-math-dunbar-number-friendships

Local Culture of the Small Group

A small group is comprised of a 'face-to-face community.' This is Dunbar's number. It's small enough that you know everybody, at least by sight. You might know something about each person, or a good many of them, depending on how long you've been part of the group. You also know who you *don't* know – you could recognise and point them out – and if you don't know someone, you'll know somebody who does know that person. There is nobody who is 100% a stranger to you.

This isn't to say that there aren't loners, or people who are apathetic, or have chips on their shoulder. But you can only be a "loner" or have a chip on your shoulder in the context of a group. If you're stuck on a desert island, you're not a "loner," you're just alone; and you can only have that chip if you're railing against others.

So, when you first start working at an organisation, you may know no one except the person who hired you. But then as you attend meetings, spend some time in the break room or at the copier, you start to get to know other people, maybe just by sight at first. And as you continue to see and interact with other people, you begin to find out a bit more about some people. The more meetings you go to and the more people you speak with, the more you know about them, even if it is just their faces, their names, where they're based, and whether they have kids or not. But, you also start to know whom to turn to with specific questions. You'll know who to go to in an emergency. You'll know who to go to if you have an idea or plan or need some back up. People also start to know what they could turn to you for.

However, it's not just a simple system of cooperation – you scratch my back, I'll scratch yours. There's another important element at work in the small group. Say, for example, that there are three people who have a lot of information about something you need. The person you'll go to is the person you know best or feel most comfortable with. So your *relationship* leads you to interact with them, not their function, not just what they know. This means you are now making decisions based upon a whole raft of social needs as well as functional needs. You'll know who you want to have lunch with, or perhaps meet up with outside of work.

And of course being part of a small group doesn't necessarily mean everything is about peace and harmony. There are negatives to a small group – there can be gossip, people may be nosy, you will probably have to interact with people you don't like, and so on. So, you'll also know exactly who you don't like and want nothing to do with.

It's the social interaction that's important. It's the *relationships* between people that are important in a small group, and it's the relationships that transform it from a faceless group to an amalgamation of individuals you know.

In a small group, you focus on interpersonal relationships to get things done – the habits, strengths and limitations, and you keep the group small enough that you can remember those things about everyone else.

A culture based on personal relationships almost always creates an environment where the same values will arise.

Values of Small Group Culture
The most important value in small group culture is, as explained above, that of building personal relationships.

Starting with the premise that those social relationships are the bedrock of small group culture, we can build a snapshot of values, behaviours and rules for the small organisation.

Value 1: Personal Relationships
Because people know each other, they are constantly strengthening the group formally and informally by

increasing awareness of people's strengths and boundaries. This allows them to create a safety net that protects against any negative results of risk-taking and innovation: because people are aware of their own habits, strengths and limitations, as well as those of others, they know who to turn to in an emergency, if a plan fails, just as they know just the right person to ask for help when creating a new project or working towards a goal.

If you have a problem with your computer, you might first ask those around you if they've had the same problem, and try to solve it that way, or you might try to look at a manual or do some research on-line. If none of those work, you would then choose help by function: hopefully anyone from the IT department would be in a position to help. If you have a good experience with that person from IT, the next time around you will probably ask to speak to the same person: you're starting to build a personal relationship.

Similarly, if you are creating new software, or a strategy for building your customer base, you might select someone who has been through this process before. And the only way you could know that is if you know the experiences, as well as skills, knowledge and aptitudes, of your colleagues.

Value 2: Weak Hierarchies and Flexibility
In small organisations, people often move around depending upon the situation, and where their skills or strengths are needed, so hierarchies may be weak. This means that it is unlikely that there will be a command-and-control type leader. Someone may take the lead on one project, but take a back seat or provide support on another, so that the most appropriate person is leading. Small group culture relies on the *flexibility* of its members to take on roles as necessary.

Weak hierarchies also require time: they're predicated upon relationships that have been built not in hours, but over weeks, months and years. Part of building those relationships is the ability to move fluidly, to be willing to take the lead or take the back seat as necessary. There is no room here for people who put ego above and beyond everything else – especially the success of the company.

And, because any member of a small group culture will have invested a great deal of time and effort into making their connections, it means that starting over at a new place would mean throwing out that investment. So, there is often a great amount of loyalty to the small group – individual members will see their futures as aligned with the future of the group and will work to take on roles that will help maintain the success of the group over time.

Value 3: Risk-Taking
Personal relationships are the most important value in small group culture; this encourages people to rely on each other and to move from role to role, within weak hierarchies.

If people are aware of strengths and limitations, and if there is a one-to-one correlation between organisational culture and values, roles and rules, then employees can create a good framework for weighing decisions in terms of uncertainty. Because there is a good framework – a safety net – in place for analysing uncertainty, employees in a small group culture will in turn be encouraged to take **risks** and **experiment**.

At the American online shoe retailer Zappos, "employees are encouraged to take appropriate risks in order to find the best way to 'deliver WOW through service.'" Risk is mitigated by an understanding of the culture: "Shared values and the right training, rather than strict rules or management approval, inform their decisions and behavior."[6]

---

[6] Anne Perschel. 'Work-Life Flow: How Individuals, Zappos, and Other Innovative Companies Achieve High Engagement.' *Global Business and Organizational Excellence*. Wiley Publications. 29:5 (2010), 29

To the outside observer, these choices might seem risky, but, the individual worker will have measured them in terms of risk and contingency and will have made an informed decision.

Value 4: Innovation
Of course, when risk-taking or experimentation are seen to have succeeded, they are just called **innovation.** Over time, flawed risk-taking and experimentation will put an organisation out of business, and so will be discouraged. But those organisations where it is successful will build a culture that nurtures innovation and flexibility amongst its staff, and those traits will not only be highly valued, but will in fact be seen as essential for the success of the organisation.

Because of values mentioned above – the importance of personal relationships, weak hierarchies, flexibility and risk-taking – the culture of the small group provides a fertile ground for innovation, as people move fluidly between roles, assessing risk and pulling together people whose skills, knowledge and aptitude make sense for different projects.

This is not a new idea. In *Drive*, Daniel Pink gives the example of William McKnight, the president and chairman of American company 3M during the 1930s and 1940s. His philosophy at work was: "hire good people and leave them alone."[7] He actively encouraged his staff to spend 15 per cent of their time on their own projects. One of his employees came up with an innovation during his 15 per cent time that many of us probably could not imagine living without today: Post-it notes.

Many companies use this strategy today – Google, for example, gives its employees 20 per cent of their time to work on their own projects – that's a day a week.

---

[7] Pink, 95.

It's the same with teams. Give them the autonomy to come up with ideas – within the context of company strategy (sphere 1) and their own individual habits, strengths and limitations (sphere 2) – and innovation will thrive.

The Values of Small Group Culture Strengthen the Group

The investment in personal relationships means that people have a vested interest in the ability of the *group* to function effectively and efficiently so it survives over the long-term. In return, a strong group sustains and supports its members.

One characteristic of a workplace with high engagement is that the workplace is seen as a group that people belong to. An unspoken goal of the engaged workplace is to **humanise** the work experience, because this strengthens the group.

This will only work, of course, if the individual members feel engaged in the group. When a small group consists of actively engaged members, it can be an effective team, using its values of flexibility and risk-taking to innovate and survive, adapting to both external and internal challenges.

Small Group Culture is defined by the fact that people know each other so...

- o They know who they can (and can't) rely on in different situations and for different things
- o Individual strengths and weaknesses are recognised; Members know each others' boundaries (significantly different from the Golden Rule)
- o People / job descriptions adapt to different situations, taking advantage of strengths
- o Hierarchies shift accordingly, or are not finely tuned
- o **Risk-taking, innovation** and **flexibility** are not just possibilities, but desired values
- o Future orientation is in terms of the group (where is the group going?) - people have a vested interest in the group's future – in other words they are engaged with it

---

Implications of Small Group Culture: Building an Effective Team

Managers and HR
For managers and HR, this leads to two criteria, which should shape your approach to finding staff. The first is: know your people. The second is: understand local culture – in a small group, relationships, flexibility and innovation will almost always be very important values.

Getting to know your people starts at the recruitment stage:
o Recruit people who are flexible in their approach, and not fully dependent upon structure to get their work done
o Design recruitment criteria to plug the gaps in teams (know your staff, so you know who you have already, and therefore who you need)

You can improve the teams you already have by improving channels of communication and increasing transparency:
o Better information-sharing between silos
o Better information-sharing between staff and line managers
  ▪ Decreases suspicion of management decision-making
  ▪ Improved people response to management
o Clear policy to reward and discipline and beyond
o Clear responsibility and accountability
o More efficient and effective processes

Employees and Potential Employees
For employees (and potential employees), the framework of the small group culture, with its values of personal relationships, weak hierarchies, risk-taking, innovation and flexibility, also has ramifications.

Because people understand each other, there will be an increased ability on the part of teams to function well through:

- o Ensuring that the development of team goals is linked to corporate goals
- o The effective setting of goals, based on their accurate knowledge of the knowledge, skills and aptitudes available within the group
- o Having a greater scope to make decisions because they have a framework for measuring risk based on the culture and people around them
- o Increased confidence of employees that they are doing the right things
- o People knowing what they're good at and opting in to projects that they can improve
- o People becoming more responsible and accountable to their colleagues, and also to the organisation as a whole

The goal is to create an atmosphere where self-managing teams can operate, where employees are able to put together their own effective teams, through self-nomination. Individuals could also start to see what knowledge, skills and aptitudes they would really need to make their teams function well, and could either identify their own development needs, or help with suggesting what would help in terms of recruitment.

Ultimately, this will have an impact on reaching goals:
- o Continuous improvement of products, services and business operations
- o Team-working, collaboration and problem solving lead to innovation
- o Continuous improvement embedded in the culture
- o Improvement of customer service

And finally, the flexible, risk-taking small group culture is resilient enough to handle change – change is in its very nature, after all. So the small group becomes the right place to tackle the changes, merges and culture clashes caused by transitions.

Going beyond the organisation walls, because the team is self-nominating, it also becomes the right place to go to in order to determine CSR projects (they'll know what they want to do) and to determine any gaps that can be filled through external networks.

In other words, the self-nominating team with a strong small group culture can diagnose its own strengths and problems, and so help the employer help the team.

Chapter 4
The Fourth Sphere
The Network – We're All Connected

> ➤ *Is engagement different for big groups than it is for small groups?*
> ➤ *Is hierarchy ever a good thing?*
> ➤ *How can a company spread over continents maintain connection and engagement?*

By all accounts, Nicholas Leeson, the so-called rogue trader who brought down Barings Bank in 1995, was a force to be reckoned with. He was young, creative and a risk-taker. In a recent BBC radio programme called *The Reunion*,[1] Leeson's then boss Peter Norris described him as 'the king of the trading floor'. Norris woefully added, "sometime after the collapse, I remember watching a video of the floor, and there was just something about your body language, and the way you were doing it – you could tell from the way other people were looking at you. I thought to myself at the time, if I'd seen this, if I'd been there – if other people had been there – we might have thought – what's all this about?"

You will recognize Leeson's traits as ideal for the small company, as described in the last chapter. In a small

---

[1] Sue MacGregor. 'Barings Bank Collapse.'
  http://www.bbc.co.uk/programmes/b0132026 12 August 2011

company, those traits would have been held in check, because his colleagues would have known him very well and might have recognised the warning signs, and company structure would have had the flexibility to absorb risk. Small teams are very good at managing the risk-takers. Working within a small team, he might have realised the impact his actions would have on his immediate colleagues. Chances are, he would have felt like he fit in with a small team – if not, he probably wouldn't have continued working there. As it was, Leeson described himself in an interview with *The Square Mile* in 2011 as "a strange City boy because I never really enjoyed the people who I worked with.... It was very much just a job. And I could not get away from it quick enough and just get home to friends in Watford, and go out. I just didn't really gel with the people." [2] He specifically contrasts working at Barings and Morgan Stanley with his experience at his first job in London, at Coutts: "Now, Coutts was slightly different. Coutts was down to earth. We used to do things like go ten-pin bowling and get pissed-up, and you'd end up missing your stop on the way home." The allegiance he might have had to a small company was not in place at Barings – asked by the BBC's Sue MacGregor what he thought about the people who would lose money because of him, he responded "It's not something I consciously thought of at the time. I suppose I was very blinkered by attempting to extract myself from the situation."

This small team was replicated in Singapore. Once he became a trader (he had originally been a bookkeeper), he protected his team. "At the weekends I'd spend a bit more time with the locals, and they were people who worked outside of the financial industry, and a lot of the people who were working for me became a lot of the people I would socialise with outside of work, so it became a little bit, incestuous isn't the word, but it blurred the definition

[2] Martin Deeson. 'Leeson Returns: Original Rogue Trader.'
http://issuu.com/squareupmedia/docs/sm_61/33 August 2011.

between employer and employee."

Leeson said he never thought he'd break the bank – in the BBC programme, he said, "not once did I think the bank would collapse. I don't think I knew what the bank was worth." This was much less likely to happen in a smaller, localised organisation. But at Barings, Leeson claimed he had no idea how much money there was. "Every time I'm asking for money from London it's coming," Leeson said. "So I don't perceive that there're any money worries and I don't perceive that the bank are having any difficulties in that regard.... You become very blinkered as to what's going on. You don't know quite what the impact is on you or on your organisation."

For many of us, it's just human nature to act as if we are in a small group – once you are in a big group, there have to be a great deal of checks and balances in place to control for this. This might take the form of technology – for example, risk management services – it might take the form of rules and regulation and compliance. Another system of checks and balances is human – putting in place a hierarchy where people are accountable down the line. Leeson's former boss, Norris, said in the BBC's *The Reunion*, "what I now realise is that... fraud is an endemic feature of commercial life, not just investment banking... the academic studies tell you that between 3 and 4% of all people will commit fraud if presented with the opportunity and the motivation." The actions of any given individual who *might* commit fraud have to be offset by a whole set of tactics to mitigate for fraud.

Leeson was working for a multinational where the appropriate checks and balances were not in place to mitigate for his actions. Those that were in place were broken. As Peter Norris described it, Barings was also going through a huge change in the 1980s and 1990s. There was a new business model, reliant upon using capital, rather than upon fees. To make matters worse, Leeson was working in the post "Big Bang" world. The Big Bang in 1986 removed the separation between "stock brokers and jobbers" and replaced making deals by shouting across the trading floor with electronic screens. In the *Square Mile* interview, Leeson described Barings as "very much a type of sink or swim kind of operation. I don't think I know of anybody who went on a training course for anything. I don't think there was any sort of HR department. I think there was just one person for about 5000 employees. It wasn't structured." The hierarchy was weak: he was based in Singapore while his bosses were in London, and because he seemed to be bringing in record profits, the system was further weakened, by allowing him to have a dual role as trader and back office manager – normally separate roles held by different people. In other words, he was meant to be his own risk manager, providing his own checks and balances. As John Gapper,[3] who wrote a book about the collapse of Barings, called *All that Glitters,* said: "No matter how good the systems a bank has in place to prevent its traders going off the rails (and Barings' controls... were notably bad), traders will always make losses and try to gamble their way out."

By the end, when Leeson was arrested and sent to jail, he had lost £827 million, and Barings Bank had collapsed, impacting many shareholders and many of Leeson's colleagues, as well as the men who ran the bank. "Ultimately," said Leeson, "I'll be remembered for my biggest failure."

The lesson here is that the values that work in a small team can ultimately lead to disaster in a large organisation. Large organisations have a different culture to small ones, and they must live by different values and rules.

---

[3] John Gapper and Madsen Pirie. 'The Human Lesson of Nick Leeson's Fraud.' http://www.ft.com/cms/s/0/00652538-808c-11d9-bed2-00000e2511c8.html#axzz1WJOXNtEw 17 February 2005

Yet the lesson never seems to be learned, at least not by the banks. French bank Société Géneral arrested their rogue trader, Jérome Kerviel, who lost £4 billion, in January of 2008. French regulators found that the checks and balances needed were not in place and fined the bank. In September of 2011, UBS trader Kweku Adoboli was arrested after he lost the Swiss bank £1.5 billion in unauthorised trades. A special committee was investigating how UBS failed to notice what Adoboli was up to.

The Fifth Sphere: Life in Large Groups
The last century has seen the growth of several interrelated trends, which have implications for how we work.
The first is that corporations have become increasingly bigger. Many people work in organisations where they can't possibly all know each other, not even by sight. They may not work in the same building, let alone the same country.

A second trend is the way technology is changing the way in which we live. Of course, this is tied to the first trend, as it is technology that allows people spread across continents to work together.

Yet, for the greater part of our history, people have lived in small groups, usually families or extended families. As we saw in the last chapter, we function most effectively in small groups. Small groups have a shared culture that makes it easy to understand each other.

The two trends have complicated our lives. As people move around for work, we have become a society of strangers, from different places, with different values, rules and roles.

Technology has allowed connection amongst the isolated individuals living in cities. But, some would argue that technology exacerbates the ever-intensifying focus on individual experience – isolated from our families and living amongst strangers, moving around the globe for work, alone in front of our touchscreens – each individual starts to become centre-stage in their own imagining. Extreme consumerism and the so-called "me generation" are logical outcomes.

The question is, without a shared culture, how can a society of strangers survive?

The challenge is to find a way to re-introduce shared values, roles and rules into the large group, to engage individuals in the bigger picture.

To understand how to engage people in the large group, we have to examine what will bring the large group together, and we need to understand its culture. What, then, are the shared values, rules and roles of the large group?

Culture of the Large Group
Large groups function differently from small groups, and so they will have different values, and rely on different behaviours and rules.

As soon as the group becomes large enough that there are strangers, things change from the way they are in small groups. If people try to function the same way as a small group, they will have to spend a lot more time maintaining social ties to incorporate all those strangers, and so they will have a lot less time to spend on trying to achieve goals. This can't be maintained if objectives are to be achieved. As we saw in the last chapter, Dunbar's number suggests that we can't really know more than hundred and fifty people.

When the numbers of people in the group start to increase, you might know that other people in the group exist, but you might know nothing else about them; you might not even know what they look like. They might not even live in the same country as you do, in the case of a multinational corporation. Still, you believe they are there. It's similar to how you take for granted that there are roughly 60 million people living in the UK, but you don't know most of them. Just because you don't know them doesn't mean that you doubt their existence. You're united only by a shared nationality and its values. In business, the organisation's shared mission and vision unite the group, sometimes across the world.[4]

When you have a large network like this, where most of the members outside your own circle are for all intents and purposes *imagined*, you deal with them by their function, rather than as another person, where you might have shared interests or friends in common.

For example, you would never call up the person who shipped your books from Amazon and thank them. You're both part of the same network, yet you would never invite them over for a cup of tea. Why not? Because you don't – and really can't – know them.

In a large enough organisation, you might not know anything about the person who helps you with IT, and someone else from IT can easily replace them, because your reason for interacting with them is simply for their function. This has implications in terms of organisational culture and values.

Large Groups at Work - values
When people don't know each other, a large organisation will have infrastructure in place to make sure that business as usual is maintained or improved. These should translate into organisational values. Normally, in a large organisation, these values will be: highly structured roles, with little room for flexibility; a strong hierarchy; an emphasis on technology and rules; and stability.

---

[4] Benedict Anderson. *Imagined Communities: Reflections on the Origin and Spread of Nationalism*. London: Verso. 1983.

In other words, the values of large groups all provide a system of checks and balances to mitigate against individual human agency and flaws.

Value 1: Highly Structured Roles
In order for a large organisation to be effective, each role has to be rigidly defined in terms of how it helps achieve the organisational goals. Individual strengths and skills are slotted in. They're the only things that are important about the person doing the job from an organisational standpoint.

Each individual, as a result, has a well-defined job description, and they are part of a department or division that also has a clear set of goals. In other words, an organisation has to have more of an assembly-line approach to creating order, so that managers, line managers, HR, and other staff all have clear-cut roles. The same goes for different departments and divisions.

This feeds into the wider organisational goals, all the way to the top. In the most extreme situation, if any one individual or department doesn't fulfil the requisite requirements of the job, the whole structure could collapse. Additionally, if an individual doesn't fulfil the requirements of the job for whatever reason, he or she can be replaced by someone who does. Equally, when a worker leaves the organisation, somebody else will be found who fits the role. Roles are rigidly defined; workers are seen as replaceable components.

Value 2: Strong Hierarchies
This naturally leads to organising the different roles and departments – think about an organisational chart, which clearly lays out the importance of different roles from top to bottom. You need a strong hierarchy based on *roles* rather than individual strengths.

This means that each role and each department have very clear-cut responsibilities. The hierarchy also provides a form of security – each worker can show that they have achieved their concrete tasks, and it is easy to identify where breakdowns in the order have occurred.

Value 3: Emphasis on Technology and Rules

Much like the above values, rules are clearly defined so as to help people attain their goals, and to enable people to know who to turn to.

A great deal of emphasis will also be placed on technology – vast computer systems, for example, to back up all the data and information generated by so many workers is essential, especially if workers are perceived as replaceable – in order to help new workers slot in and replace others. They need access to what their predecessors have done and they need rules to help guide them on how to continue on in their role.

Technology provides security, improves communications, and streamlines change, locally and across continents.

Value 4: Stability

The repercussion of the three values listed above is that, unlike in a smaller organisation, there can be no risk-taking on the individual level, because if you don't know everyone else's habits, strengths and limitations, you can't assess the knock-on effects of risk-taking. This makes perfect sense for a large organisation where people don't know each other.

These values act as mechanisms to increase stability, in a setting where the actions of any one individual could have a large destabilising effect. The story of Nick Leeson is a good example; and it's a story that has happened time and again for the same reason: the factors and rules that create systems of checks and balances to ensure stability were broken. Jerome Kerviel, who had started working for the French bank Société Général in 2000, committed fraud that ended up costing the bank £3.7 billion. His actions were only uncovered in 2008. As a BBC article[5] put it at the time, "Société Général said the trader had taken what it called 'massive fraudulent directional positions in 2007 and 2008 beyond his limited authority.'" And in September of 2011, UBS trader Kweku Adoboli engaged in unauthorised trades that cost the bank £1.5 billion. Not only had these men acted beyond the constraints of their roles and broken the rules, but they had also rocked the stability of the organisations, and those organisations couldn't absorb the shock.

Stability, then, is an important value for large organisations. Large organisations maintain stability through rigid adherence to *roles and hierarchies*. They also introduce many rules and as much *technology* as possible to help build a strong frame for those social roles. Being able to *play by the rules* is therefore also a strongly valued trait in employees.

Network (or Large Group) Culture is defined by the fact that people don't know each other so...

o   There has to be strict adherence to roles and rules
o   Technology is important for building a strong infrastructure and keeping track of data – you can't rely on individuals to be there for a long time and remember things
o   Hierarchies are strict and well-defined
o   **Stability** and **playing by the rules** are not just possibilities, but desired values
o   Future orientation is in terms of the individual (where am I going?) – work is just a stop along the their own path – they may change jobs often in keeping with how they want their lives to go

---

[5] 'Rogue trader to cost SocGen $7bn'
   http://news.bbc.co.uk/1/hi/7206270.stm January 2008.

Implications of Large Group Culture: Engaging the Network

Managers and HR
The approach to engaging staff in a large group is, as you might expect, different to that of a small group. In addition to all the small face-to-face groups that may form, the challenge is to make sure that people across floors, building or countries can create networks of knowledge, information and skills that will contribute to the strengthening of the organisation.

Start by recruiting people who are a cultural fit for a large organisation. In other words, choose people who:
o Have an ability to plug into the organisation's infrastructure
o Can work well within strictly defined roles and hierarchies
o Will contribute to stability
o Like to play by the rules

Work to improve the possibility of strong internal networks being formed – in other words, create small face-to-face groups within the larger group:
o Eliminate faceless bureaucracy: even if bureaucracy can't be done away with, it doesn't have to be faceless - clarify the line of communication so people can easily know who to turn to for what
o Information-sharing between silos – make sure people know not only where their own roles begin and end, but where they fit into the bigger picture: they'll know who to talk to beyond their own team to get things done
o Put in place the communication channels which will allow people to connect with like-minded people (for example, consider social media)
o Move from tea & toilets to strategy – better integration and inclusion of staff, so they are working together to help maintain or improve strategy

Build strong external networks:
o Improve relationships with external partners
o Create a frame of reference – i.e. CSR success stories – see how other organisations handle things – connect with them
o External partners in terms of CSR

Maintaining or improving business as usual will be an outcome of:
o Improving communication between people who might not normally interact because they don't share office space
o Understanding and managing expectations, both in terms of what is expected of staff, and in terms of what they can expect from the organisation, in terms of culture and values
o Ensuring people understand where they fit into the big picture

Employees and Potential Employees
For employees (and potential employees), large group culture, with its values of stability, structure, hierarchy, and strict roles, can provide security, though it can also feel constraining.

Because people don't know each other each other, there will be a need to increase networking through:
o Using technology – like social media – to remove local boundaries
o Making sure people understand the line of command so they know exactly what they're accountable for and why

The goal is to ensure that each employee understands the big picture so they can move through it with the information they need to make sense of their job and who to turn to for any information about the things they might need to do their job.

Chapter 5
The Fifth Sphere
Society

> ➢ *Can doing good and doing business go hand-in-hand?*
> ➢ *How are business and society interrelated?*

People should do good for the sake of doing good, but companies shouldn't.

Now before you jump out of your seat and hit the panic button, what I mean to say is that companies should do good because ultimately, for the long-term, it's actually in their interest to do so. A 2014 McKinsey article by Eric Beinhocker and Nick Hanauer[1] suggests that we redefine capitalism – instead of being driven by shareholder profit, they see capitalism as a mechanism of creation. In *Redefining Capitalism,* they propose that we replace GDP as a measure of prosperity with a new measure: "Ultimately," they say, "the measure of the wealth of a society is the range of human problems it has solved and how available it has made those

---

[1] Eric Beinhocker and Nick Hanauer. 'Redefining Capitalism.' http://www.mckinsey.com/insights/corporate_social_responsibility/redefining_capitalism September 2014.

solutions to its people." And, what else is business if not the solving of human problems?

We've been living in an era of short-termism, where a large amount of the focus is on delivering annual profits, improving share values and the pay out of dividends to shareholders.

But an intelligent company knows that to exist in the future means you must be aware of what you're doing in the present. Today's actions have consequences. And a truly intelligent company knows that it is a part of society. It's in the best interest of companies to make sure that society is healthy and working well so that they'll have employees with the right skills, and competitors who challenge them and ensure their products are the best, and they'll have communities who need and can afford their products. If they in any way act destructive towards society, rather than nurturing it, they will in the long-term destroy themselves too. As Beinhocker and Hanauer say, "the crucial contribution business makes to society is *transforming ideas into products and services that solve problems.*"

In fact, failing to take part in society and failing to improve it are sure-fire ways for a company to eventually fail itself. Providing solutions is growth not just for companies, but for society too.

Altruism's got nothing to do with it...
Recently, I was training a group at a large multinational. This was the second time I'd come in, and we were exploring their rights under TUPE (Transfer of Undertakings Protection of Employees). In this situation, their part of the company had been sold off, and the employees were ring-fenced in as part of that sale. In other words, it wasn't just the equipment or the workspace, or the locale that the buyer was interested in: they also were buying the employees' expertise and experience.

One of the attendees was a fairly young man. He was upset because he couldn't understand why his company was selling him on. He wasn't being remotely arrogant. The way he explained it was that he had been with the company since he was 17 years old. Before he'd been hired, he had thought nobody would have him and that he wasn't clever enough to go to university. And so, when he and many of his friends were recruited, it felt like a lifesaver. As a result, he was incredibly loyal to the company, and would have been happy to work for them until he retired. He couldn't understand why the company was no longer loyal to him, as he was to it.

It was as if the company were a person, a loved one, who no longer loved him back, which led him to having a great feeling of betrayal and rejection. This was the source of his disbelief. What had changed?

We talked about the company having to make decisions that would ensure its success and existence in the future, showing that it wasn't personal. He knew that he would have a job, and because of the TUPE agreement, that his terms and conditions wouldn't change. But none of this mattered. He couldn't see past the fact that they didn't want him anymore.

Realigning expectations
The problem, on the face of it, is a simple one.

It's about aligning two different cultural systems – human society and the corporate environment. In the best of all possible worlds, they would both revolve around the same four values:
1. Long-termism
2. Fairness
3. Taking care of the environment
4. Prioritising the many over the few

Human Society

Human relationships are quite often predicated upon reciprocity and our values usually revolve around a primary axis of fairness and trust. So if you value loyalty, you'll surround yourself with people you consider loyal. If you have a strong work ethic, you'll probably prefer to work with others who share that drive. And so on. You'll try to do good for your friends and family, so that you can maintain those relationships well into the future. Extrapolate this to the wider group, and this is *society.*

Any society needs the following four values to survive:

Value 1: Long-termism

The goal is the continued existence of the society or culture long into the future. The ideal is for society to take care of its members, though this often falls apart or is torn apart by individuals driven by self-interest. But it's why here in the UK, for example, we have the NHS and there is access to free education until university. Through our taxes, we take care of those less able to take care of themselves, ensuring that as a society, we all benefit.

Value 2: Fairness

In order to become invested in society, the members need to feel that it is fair, so that everyone is treated equally. This is different than saying there shouldn't be hierarchies or segmentation; rather hierarchies based on merit are fair, but those based on, say, accident of birth (like aristocracy) are not. A fair society doesn't have hierarchies based on accidents of birth. As long as segmentation is not used to discriminate but to help, then that can be fair as well (for example, women may need different healthcare than men).

Value 3: Taking care of the environment

Because societies have an in-built desire to last over the long-term, they will consider their environment or die out. Jared Diamond has a great story about Easter Island, which was once a lush and prosperous island, but due to an increasing interest in individual status and a lack of understanding of the environment, has now become a desolate and desiccated place, home mostly to the gigantic stone heads for which the island has come to be known. He asks, what did the islander who cut down the very last tree think?[2]

Value 4: Prioritising the many over the few

After World War II ended, the British introduced the welfare system that we now have. Its goal was to provide a level playing field; to ensure that as many people as possible are educated, that people would have both preventative and curative healthcare, a warm home and enough food.

Basically, the welfare system was made to address the lowest two levels of Maslow's hierarchy of needs – physiological needs and the need for safety – which he had proposed in 1943. The logic is that by providing for these two needs, any individual member of society could then participate in the three top levels: love and belonging; esteem; and self-actualisation.

These four values are what we expect society to provide us with. The social contract is that we then become fully functioning members of society. Of course, there are flaws in this idea. There are many people who fall between the cracks for many different reasons, and society should be there to provide a safety net, but it doesn't always work the way it ought to. Still, you might say that its heart is in the right place.

What about the ethos of the company? What is the core around which it rotates and what are its related values?

---

[2] Jared Diamond. *Collapse*. London: Penguin Books. 2005

The Company

It might surprise you to find out that companies share these same values. However, the spoken premise – improve business as usual so the company can survive long into the future – is often at odds with an unspoken premise (that most of us are aware of): to maximise shareholder wealth. And it is this unspoken premise that actually provides the values that put companies in conflict with society.

Value 1: Long-termism

As discussed in chapter 1, the bottom line for all companies is to survive. Thus, the way to achieve this to constantly be coming up with and adjusting strategies in order to adapt to the constant changes in both the world around companies and to internal changes.

The ideal is for a company to stay afloat through time, so it can continue to make money for its shareholders – an add-on is that through strong strategy, employees profit as well, since it ensures that they have jobs. But where the individual might see loyalty as a long-term relationship between two parties, the company sees loyalty as whatever is necessary to ensure its own existence going forward. Again, this isn't a bad thing – the better the company does, the more it can afford to keep employees on and bring in new ones.

That's the ideal. But if shareholders' needs are prioritised over the company's long-term health, then the real value, the unspoken value, becomes to make as much of a profit in the short-term as possible to pay out to shareholders. In this scenario long-term strategies are sacrificed for short-term gain, to the future expense of shareholders, and the immediate expense of employees. It would be interesting to know how often this *actually* happens, and how often this is just the *perception* of why change occurs.

Value 2: Fairness

For the company, fairness also means equality and merit-based reward, however, unlike society, fairness is tethered to strategy. In other words, fairness must always be looked at through the lens of what is good for the company. This does mean that sometimes the jobs or benefits of some have to be sacrificed for the company to continue to exist in the long-term. Fairness here is not about everyone being treated the same (indeed it should never mean that – remember that the Golden Rule is deeply flawed), as it might for society. For society, it is irrelevant whether the person receiving social housing is a good or kind person or not, or what kinds of skills they have, as this moral is predicated on need. For a company, it's not the same: of course redundancy shouldn't be based on a person's character, but it is absolutely based upon their skills, and on whether their continued employment fits in with company strategy for survival. Again, it's based on the company's need to achieve its strategic goals.

Of course, the reality can be different. If shareholders are prioritised over employees and society, this often leads to unfair treatment – whether this is reflected in pay differentials, or the abuse of people in sweatshop conditions. If people feel they're being treated unfairly, they will become less productive, which will not benefit the shareholders in the long-term.

Value 3: Taking care of the environment

The environment is all we have. Without a functioning environment, there is no future for companies or people. On some level, companies understand this. There are all sorts of campaigns, for example, by companies like BP to find alternative sources of energy.

Encouragingly, there are real signs too of a deep-seated, long-term interest in the environment, both physical and social. In 2010, a new kind of corporation was created in the

United States – the certified B ("benefit") Corp. These are "a new type of corporation which uses the power of business to solve social and environmental problems." As of 2014, there are over 1000 certified B Corporations in more than 30 countries and 60 industries.[3]

To receive certified B Corporation status, a company must:
1. Meet comprehensive and transparent social and environmental performance standards;
2. Meet higher legal accountability standards;
3. Build business constituency for public policies that support sustainable business.

It's a start. But there are no really big names signed up for B Corp status (yet!). It seems that for a great number of companies, when it comes to the environment, the status quo is good enough.

Value 4: Prioritise the many over the few
In keeping with the idea that strategies should be developed to ensure the long-term survival of a company, the associated value is that the overall survival of the company – the many – is more important than that of a few individuals' needs.

And more and more companies understand that they are rooted in society, and that therefore a healthy society that works well is essential to their own well-being. A healthy society means that businesses will have employees with the right skills, and competitors who challenge them and ensure their products are the best, and they'll have communities who need and can afford their products. If companies in any way act destructive towards society in the short-term, rather than nurturing it, they will in the long-term destroy themselves too.

---

[3] 'The Non-Profit Behind B Corps.' http://www.bcorporation.net/about

In fact, failing to take part in society and failing to improve it are sure-fire ways for a company to eventually fail itself.

Engagement for the Long-Term

A good example is the story of Siemens, a leading global engineering and technology services company. Brian Holliday, the Divisional Director of Industry Automation at Siemens' Birmingham office, had identified that there would be a definite shortage of engineers in the future.

Siemens' solution was a perfect mix of doing good for society and doing good for the company, using the values of long-termism. In other words, Siemens solved their business problem at the same time as they solved a problem for society. They started to help develop those future engineers by going into local schools. As Holliday said:

"At Siemens we have been working with local schools, driving work experience initiatives, supporting a vibrant graduate scheme, delivering mentor programmes, as well as financially supporting the Newcastle and Nottingham University-based E3 Academy, to try and address the ongoing challenge the industry faces."[4]

As a result, young students in Birmingham have hope for jobs at a time when youth unemployment is incredibly high. They're engaged with Siemens and they don't even work there. Their community will see it as truly doing good - the students may or may not go on to work for Siemens, they're of course free to take those skills elsewhere. And Siemens ensures that it'll be there in the long run, because it will have a workforce with the right skills – after all, they helped train them.

Altruism's got nothing to do with it.

---

[4] Brian Holliday. 'Engineering for Prosperity.'
http://www.industry.siemens.co.uk/home/uk/en/IADT/news/Pages/Engineer
ingforProsperiety.aspx 8 October 2010.

And the Siemens story is one of many. There's the story of Intuit in a *New York Times* story from 2011,[5] which lets millions of low-income Americans file their taxes for free, knowing that many of them will become paying customers. The founder of Intuit, Scott Cook, said "We look for places we can use our strengths as a company to help solve big problems. You can call that shared value if you like. But I look at it as the business we're in." Or General Electric, who used new green technology to lower the cost for their clients and meet the requirements of the government, ending up with a resulting environmental benefit. GE's chief executive said it had nothing to do with corporate social responsibility: "We did it from a business standpoint from Day 1."

Even if you accept the premise that companies are there to make money for their shareholders, long-termism will always make more sense than short-termism, and solving problems for society means greater profit for shareholders. The two go hand-in-hand.

Aligning the Culture of the Organisation with that of Society
This means organising companies around the basic principal of long-term good for the community, which derives from that which will provide long-term benefit for the company:

o Think about the long-term: provide training for future employees (or funding for training, or personnel to do the training etc.)
o Think about fairness: individuals need to ask the right questions to understand why companies do what they do, change ought to be about long-term survival
o Think about the environment: if there's no environment, there's no business.
o Think about the many: self-interest won't help the company over the long-term.

---

[5] Steve Lohr. 'First, Make Money. Also, Do Good.'
   http://www.nytimes.com/2011/08/14/business/shared-value-gains-in-corporate-responsibility-efforts.html?pagewanted=all August 2011

PART TWO:

Engagement Toolkit

Engagement in the First Sphere:
Helping Individuals Understand the Strategic Narrative

This is a set of questions for management to answer, which should outline for staff the strategic narrative around change, so they can plug themselves and any concerns they have into that broader picture. The questions fall into five categories: core, timeline, measuring success, contingency and risk, communication strategies.

These questions are a reference tool – how would you use them in your organisation? What questions would you add?

Core questions:
1. What is the trigger for change?*
2. What is your strategy for addressing the need for change?*
3. What other options did you consider?*
4. Why did you reject those other options?*
5. Who's involved in decision-making?

Timeline questions:
1. When will the change take place?
2. When will implementation be considered complete?
3. Is this part of a longer-term project – are there other phases?
4. How long ago did you identify the business objective?
5. Is there consultation? If so, what is the timeline?

Measuring success questions:
1. What does success look like?
2. What are the key milestones?
3. What system do you have in place to measure success?
4. Have you used it before and how did it work?
5. What is the timeline for measuring success?

Contingency / risk questions:
1. What is Plan B?
2. What were the key findings of your risk analysis?
3. What are the knock-on effects to other areas of the business?*
4. Can we see your risk analysis?*
5. Have you considered how disengagement might impact on the change process?*

Communication Strategy questions:
1. What is your communication strategy?
2. Are there phases in your communication strategy and what are they?
3. What is your plan for dealing with upset or resentful staff?*
4. Who will be involved in the communication process?
5. What system do you have in place to ensure that your communication is clear and understandable to your audience?

From the IPA's 15 Questions

Engagement in the Second Sphere:
Self-Awareness at Work Checklist

Work itself is different for everyone. But, creating the environment
for engaging with work can be addressed with consistency. Share it
with anyone who you need to work with, so you manage their
expectations.

Set the scene for work – what are your habits:
✓ Do you need a tidy work environment?	□ yes	□ no
✓ What helps you focus?	□ quiet	□ noise
✓ Do you like to….	□ sit	□ stand
✓ To get a drink or snack prior to starting?	□ yes	□ no
✓ Do you need any reference materials handy?	□ yes	□ no
✓ Any tools you might need – pens, post-its, diary?	□ yes	□ no
✓ Do you have all the information you need?	□ yes	□ no
✓ When is the best time of day for you to work?	□ am	□ pm

Set boundaries to maintain self-discipline and mitigate procrastination:
□ Timer set for 20 minutes
□ List of three top things to achieve today
□ Weekly schedule planned out – top goals and related actions
□ Rewards for getting things done

Internal environment – what is your personal approach
✓ Are you an introvert or an extrovert?	□ intro	□ extro
✓ Do you work methodically?	□ yes	□ no
✓ Do you work…	□ slowly	□ quickly
✓ Do you work in…	□ bursts	□ continuously
✓ Are you a multi-tasker?	□ yes	□ no
✓ Do you work best…	□ alone	□ in a team
✓ Do you have all the necessary skills?	□ yes	□ no
✓ Or do you need some training?	□ yes	□ no
✓ Do you know people who can help?	□ yes	□ no
✓ Do you know what's expected of you?	□ yes	□ no
✓ Do you know everyone's role in your team?	□ yes	□ no

Engagement in the Third Sphere:
Analysing The Team Toolkit

This toolkit provides four sets of questions to analyse the team's understanding of strategic impact, individual characteristics, ways of working, and built in processes for reflection.

Strategic Impact
✓ We understand the organisational strategy   □ yes   □ no
✓ Our work is connected clearly to strategy   □ yes   □ no
✓ Our team's expertise contributes to strategy   □ yes   □ no
✓ We have defined our results in terms of strategy   □ yes   □ no

Within the group, each individual team member...
✓ Has the necessary skills (and if not, can upskill)   □ yes   □ no
✓ Knows the others' strengths, skills and expertise   □ yes   □ no
✓ Values the other team members   □ yes   □ no
✓ Takes the time to get to know other team members   □ yes   □ no

Ways of Working
✓ We act as a group   □ yes   □ no
✓ Therefore, we stick to the decisions of the group   □ yes   □ no
✓ We know the rules and accepted behaviours   □ yes   □ no
✓ We each consider ourselves to be equally   □ yes   □ no
   responsible in achieving the aims of the group

Reflection
✓ We review and reflect on our progress   □ yes   □ no
✓ We ask for help when we need it   □ yes   □ no
✓ We request feedback from each other   □ yes   □ no
✓ We request feedback from those outside the team   □ yes   □ no

Engagement in the Fourth Sphere:
The Network – Aligning Teams

This is about aligning your team with other teams and the broader organisational culture. So first of all, it's important to know if people understand:

- ✓ How our team works with other teams
- ✓ How our work is connected to strategy
- ✓ How work is connected to the work of other teams

To see if the team is aligned with the broader organisation:

Team		Value	Organisation	
Yes	No		Yes	No
		Roles are *clearly defined*		
		There are *strict hierarchies*		
		There is *strict adherence to rules*		
		Technology is necessary for maintaining infrastructure		
		Technology is necessary for keeping track of data		
		Stability is highly valued		
		This job might just be *one stop* in a career		
		People know each other *personally*		
		The group is *less than* 150 people		
		Personal relationships are important		
		Roles are *flexible and changeable*		

		Leadership shifts depending on the project		
		Risk-Taking is encouraged or seen as essential		
		Innovation is highly valued		

At the end of this, if your answers for the team and the organisation are opposite to each other, you know the team is not aligned with the organisation.

This is fine and in fact can be really useful – for example, you want your learning & development team to be flexible and innovative in coming up with solutions, and you wouldn't want to quash that.

However, if you've identified this disconnect, you'll want to come up with strategies for insuring that the culture of the organisation and the culture of the team are clear to each other, so that people communicate well to each other.

Engagement in the Fifth Sphere:
Toolkit for Engaging with Society

Taking as a premise the idea that companies are here to solve human problems, there are two areas where companies can act. The first is internally, and this has been addressed with the first four toolkits.

The second area is externally and is future-orientated:

Future Needs	
Strategic Narrative	What human problems is the business trying to solve?
	How does your product / service improve lives?
	At what rate are those problems solved?
Future Employees	Does your society focus on the skills you need (i.e. are future workers being trained)?
	If not, what can you do to ensure those skills will be available? (see Siemens example, Chapter 5)
	How will your employees be *creators* of solutions?
Measuring success	What are the benchmarks of success for you?
	How do they link back to the human problem you want to solve?
	Over what period of time will this take place?
Future Customers	Identify the customer for the problem you are solving
	How do you ensure that your product actually solves this customer's problem?
	What knowledge are you contributing to, to ensure you have an informed customer?

Bibliography

Anderson, Benedict. *Imagined Communities: Reflections on the Origin and Spread of Nationalism*. London: Verso. 1983.

Beinhocker, Eric and Nick Hanauer. 'Redefining Capitalism.' http://www.mckinsey.com/insights/corporate_social_responsibility /redefining_capitalism September 2014.

Berns, Gregory. *Iconoclast: A Neuroscientist Reveals How to Think Differently*. Cambridge, MA: Harvard Business School Press. 2008.

Bolchover, David. *The Living Dead: Switched Off, Zoned Out – The Shocking Truth about Office Life*. Sussex, UK: Capstone Publishing Company. 2005.

Brown, Felicity. 'Percentage of Global Population Living in Cities.' http://www.guardian.co.uk/news/datablog/2009/aug/18/percentag e-population-living-cities 24 August 2009

Buckingham, Marcus and C. Coffman. *First, Break all the Rules*. London: Pocket Books. 2005.

Capozzi, Marla M., Renée Dye, and Amy Howe. 'Sparking creativity in teams: An executive's guide.' *McKinsey Quarterly* (April 2011).

Csikszentmihalyi, Mihaly. *Flow*. London: Rider Books. 2002.

Deeson, Martin. 'Leeson Returns: Original Rogue Trader.' http://issuu.com/squareupmedia/docs/sm_61/33 August 2011.

Diamond, Jared. *Collapse: How Societies Choose to Fail or Survive*. London: Penguin Books. 2005.

Dunbar, Robin. 'Robin Dunbar on Dunbar Numbers.' http://www.socialsciencespace.com/2013/11/robin-dunbar-on-dunbar-numbers/ November 2013.

Fairlie, Paul. 'All Generations Want Meaningful Work.' *HR Reporter* (June 6, 2011).

Gapper, John and Madsen Pirie. 'The Human Lesson of Nick Leeson's Fraud.' http://www.ft.com/cms/s/0/00652538-808c-11d9-bed2-00000e2511c8.html#axzz1WJOXNtEw 17 Feb 2005.

Geirland, John. 'Go with the Flow.' *Wired Magazine*. Issue 4.09 (September 1996).

Harvey, David. *The Enigma of Capital*. London: Profile Books. 2010.

Holliday, Brian. 'Engineering for Prosperity.' http://www.industry.siemens.co.uk/home/uk/en/IADT/news/Pages/EngineeringforProsperiety.aspx 8 October 2010.

Konnikova, Maria. 'The Limits of Friendship.' http://www.newyorker.com/science/maria-konnikova/social-media-affect-math-dunbar-number-friendships 7 October 2014.

Lohr, Steve. 'First, Make Money. Also, Do Good.' http://www.nytimes.com/2011/08/14/business/shared-value-gains-in-corporate-responsibility-efforts.html?pagewanted=all Aug 2011

Lovallo, Dan and Olivier Sibony. 'Taking the Bias out of Meetings.' http://www.mckinsey.com/insights/strategy/taking_the_bias_out_of_meetings April 2010.

Lovallo, Dan and Olivier Sibony. 'The Case for Behavioural Strategy.' http://www.mckinsey.com/insights/strategy/the_case_for_behavioral_strategy March 2010.

Luckhurst, Derek. *Maintaining Workforce Engagement in an Economic Downturn*. IPA Bulletin: October 2008.

Luckhurst, Derek. *Option-Based Consultation Provides Mutual Benefits*. IPA Bulletin: March 2003.

MacGregor, Sue. 'Barings Bank Collapse.' http://www.bbc.co.uk/programmes/b0132026 12 August 2011

Macleod, David and Nita Clarke. 'Engage For Success.' http://www.engageforsuccess.org/wp-content/uploads/2012/09/file52215.pdf

Perschel, Anne. 'Work-Life Flow: How Individuals, Zappos, and Other Innovative Companies Achieve High Engagement.' *Global Business and Organizational Excellence*. Wiley Publications. 29:5 (2010), 17-30.

Pink, Daniel H. *Drive: The Surprising Truth about what Motivates Us*. Edinburgh: Canongate Books. 2010.

Pink, Daniel H. 'Employees are Faster and More Creative when Solving Other People's Problems.' *The Telegraph* 22 May 2011.

Popova, Maria. 'The Secret of Life from Steve Jobs in 46 Seconds.' http://www.brainpickings.org/2011/12/02/steve-jobs-1995-life-failure/

Robinson, Ken. *Finding Your Element: How to Discover Your Talents and Passions and Transform Your Life*. New York: Penguin Books. 2013.

Robison, Jennifer. 'Turning Around Employee Turnover.' http://www.gallup.com/businessjournal/106912/turning-around-your-turnover-problem.aspx 8 May 2008.

'Rogue trader to cost SocGen $7bn' http://news.bbc.co.uk/1/hi/7206270.stm January 2008

'Stress-related and psychological disorders in Great Britain 2014.' http://www.hse.gov.uk/statistics/causdis/stress/index.htm

'The Non-Profit Behind B Corps.' http://www.bcorporation.net/about

Tonnies, Ferdinand. *Community and Civil Society*. Cambridge: Cambridge University Press. 2001.

Yell, Graeme. 'Engagement Matters.' http://www.haygroup.com/EngagementMatters/research-findings/united-kingdom.aspx

'United Nations Population Fund' http://www.unfpa.org/pds/urbanization.htm

Acknowledgements

This book would not have come into being without the participation of the many managers, HR professionals and staff I have worked with over the years. Often during training, I have been inspired and educated; I have been moved and made to laugh. Most importantly, these ideas have been put to the test in the real world and made better.

I'd like to thank Roger Fife for all the conversations we've had about engagement and other things, and his unfaltering belief in me. This never would have happened without him. Trust me, it really wouldn't have.

Derek Luckhurst of the IPA was one of the first people I met when I moved to London. We have more or less talked about everything under the sun. He gave me a chance and taught me so much. His creativity around employee engagement has shaped my thinking extensively.

Many thanks go to my sister, Marieke Cassia Gartner, who patiently edited any number of versions of this book; her critical eye missed nothing.

Glynn Jones' deep business sense meant that the new, exciting ideas about engagement that we explored always had a solid grounding.

Philip Dundas showed me that business and changing society for the better are not antithetical. In fact, work that changes society for the better is the best kind of work.

David Zinger read several chapters – putting questions at the beginning of each chapter was his idea. He also gently guided me away from my propensity for way too much deep historical analysis.

**Notes**

Notes

<u>*Notes*</u>

<u>*Notes*</u>

Notes

9421046R00065

Printed in Great Britain
by Amazon.co.uk, Ltd.,
Marston Gate.